From Kilts to Sarongs

FROM KILTS
TO SARONGS

Scottish Pioneers of Singapore

GRAHAM BERRY

◦LANDMΔRK◦BOOKS◦

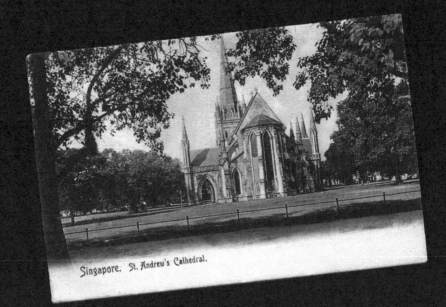

Singapore. St. Andrew's Cathedral.

To the memory of
all Scots who left their country
and never made it home again.

CONTENTS

Page 4: Picture postcard of St Andrew's Cathedral. (Private Collection)
Facing: Coffee bean batik sarong. (Ian Alexander, CC-BY-SA-3.0)

FOREWORD

IT WAS AT A LUNCH in the Churchill Room of the Tanglin Club that I suggested to the author to write a book on the history of the Scots in Singapore. I did so for three reasons.

First, I wanted Singaporeans to be more aware of the differences between the English, the Scots, the Welsh and the Irish. We have a tendency to refer to all of them as British and to use the terms, "British" and "English", interchangeably. Singaporeans have a very superficial knowledge about Scotland and the Scots. When asked to identify some unique qualities and achievements of the Scots, the Singaporean would probably refer to the bagpipe, the kilt, whisky and golf. We do not know that the Scottish Enlightenment had preceded the English Enlightenment. Nor do we know that this remarkable nation of only five million people had produced many great men such as Adam Smith, David Hume, David Livingstone, James Watt and Ian Fleming and great writers such as Robert Burns, Walter Scott, Robert Louis Stevenson and Arthur Conan Doyle.

In 2008, Rosemary Lim published a book on the Irish in Singapore entitled *An Irish Tour of Singapore*. I am glad that we will now have Graham Berry's book on the history of the Scots in Singapore.

Second, I wanted to highlight the contributions which many Scottish pioneers had made to Singapore. The first two Residents of Singapore, William Farquhar and John Crawfurd, were Scots. Indeed, of the first eight Residents of Singapore, five were Scots. The architect of the lighthouse on Pedra Branca, John Thomson, was a Scot. The lighthouse bears the name of a famous Scottish hydrographer James Horsburgh. Some of our oldest law firms such as Rodyk & Davidson, Donaldson & Birkinshaw and Drew & Napier were founded by Scottish lawyers. Some of our most famous companies such as Fraser & Neave, Sime Darby and the Straits Trading Company were founded by Scottish entrepreneurs. The HSBC and the Standard Chartered Bank were founded by the Scots.

Some of Singapore's leaders have recorded their admiration for the qualities and character of the Scots. Commenting on the dismal performance of the Allied forces against the Japanese, Mr Lee Kuan Yew said, "There were some who won my respect and admiration. Among them were the Highlanders whom I recognised by their Scottish caps. Even in defeat they held

Colonial gentleman in sarong and *tutup* jacket with his Chinese servants and Malay syce. (National Archives of Singapore)

themselves erect and marched in time." Mr S R Nathan has, in his memoirs, written admiringly of a Scottish engineer J R Spence who did not hesitate to speak up for two of his subordinates whom he felt had been unjustly dealt with. Mr Nathan wrote, "I later learnt that he was a Scot and such outspokenness was typical of them, when they saw an injustice."

Third, I wanted to draw attention to the unjust manner in which history had dealt with Singapore's first Resident and Commandant, William Farquhar. His name has practically disappeared from the history of Singapore. All the credit for the founding and subsequent success of Singapore has been given to Raffles. If Raffles was the visionary and idealist, Farquhar was the practical man of action, who turned vision to reality. Unfortunately, the two men quarrelled and Raffles summarily dismissed Farquhar in 1823.

The only legacies of Farquhar remaining in Singapore are with our National Museum. The first is a beautiful set of 477 paintings of the flora and fauna of Malacca which Farquhar had commissioned when he was the Commandant of Malacca. In 1996, Mr G K Goh bought the collection at an auction in London and donated them to the museum. The second is a silver epergne which the Chinese community had presented to Farquhar on his departure. There used to be a road named after Farquhar but it has disappeared. I think the time has come for us to restore him to our collective memory.

Tommy Koh
Ambassador-At-Large
Honorary Chairman, National Heritage Board

FOREWORD

THIS BOOK by Graham Berry is the product of an enthusiastic addiction to a place and is born out of a lifetime's experience of creativity.

Graham's distinguished career in arts administration in Scotland means that he is well known to a range of writers and artists and that he has an encyclopedic knowledge not just of culture in Scotland but of how those who create go about their business.

It was perhaps therefore inevitable that, at some stage, Graham would want to join in the creative fun and he has done so with style and substance in this examination not just of the history of Singapore but of the culture and motivation of those Scots who helped to make that history.

At the outset, the Scottish reader will discover one very tantalising fact. If Captain Alexander Hamilton had accepted the offer put to him in 1703, the success of Singapore might have redeemed the failure of Darien and created an opportunity for Scotland to establish its own mercantile empire. In his memoirs, the privateer and adventurer recalls that the Prince of Johor made him a present of "a proper place for a company to found a colony upon", lying "in the centre of trade and accommodated with good rivers and a safe harbour". That place was Singapore, but Captain Hamilton, no doubt with the live memory of his country's humiliation on the Isthmus of Panama just three years before, told the Prince it could be "of no use to a private person" and thus avoided the entanglement.

The rest is history. Scotland's failure at Darien was one (though only one) of the causes of the Union in 1707. And Singapore would have to wait more than 100 years before Sir Stamford Raffles claimed the territory, though the hard work in starting to make it a real place of promise was undertaken by another Scot, Colonel William Farquhar, who was unjustly treated by the cavalier Raffles and whose reputation is well restored by Berry.

After Farquhar, the day to day administration fell to Dr John Crawfurd, an Islay-born physician, and so the momentum of Scottish political and commercial leadership began to build and continued well into the last century.

So far, so conventional. But this is not a conventional history. Mixed in amongst the ministers, physicians, promoters of libraries, soldiers, founder of chambers of commerce, brewers, bankers, lawyers, accountants, Boys'

Brigade officers, planters, teachers, soldiers and traders is a detailed, well-informed and wide-ranging leaven of Scottish history and culture that explains and underpins the actions and motivations of all of them. This unusual approach can be challenging at times but it leaves the reader – or this reader at least – enriched with a kaleidoscope of perspectives and influences that justify Berry's conclusion that the Scots who built Singapore contributed not just economically and politically but also in terms of building the character and characteristics of the place, in a way that has contributed to its long-term success and what it is now.

That, for a Scottish reader, is another tantalising thought in the context of the referendum on Scottish Independence in 2014. For if so much could be done to make a vibrant and successfully nation on the other side of the world over so long, why could it not – indeed why should it not – be put to the same effect at home?

There are many memorable things in the book but amongst the most moving are the stories of courage during World War II. The contribution of Major Ian Stewart of the Argyll & Sutherland Highlanders (my own father's former regiment) to the brave but unsuccessful defence of the area cannot be understated but neither can the stubborn, wooden-headed and arrogant approach of those British administrators who refused to see the imperative for radical action that Stewart was trying to draw to their attention. The result of their complacence was the loss of the colony to the Japanese and the horrific forced labour, torture and imprisonment of many soldiers and civilians as well as the cruel abuse and suffering of the indigenous population.

Yet, even in defeat, the Scots had an influence as Berry illustrates with a well-chosen quote from former Premier Lee Kuan Yew that recalls the dignity of the Scottish regiments marching into captivity to the sound of the pipes playing "Heilan Laddie". And his tribute to Eric Lomax, the Edinburgh-born "Railway Man", is as timely as it is poignant.

Graham Berry has produced much more than the "modest volume", as he describes the book. It is a fascinating, diverse, rich and unusually structured volume which imparts information, entertainment and inspiration in equal measure. It should not only engage those who want to know about Singapore; it should also attract readers who wish to reflect on Scottish history, character and potential and on what has been and still can be.

Michael Russell
Member of the Scottish Parliament
Minister for Environment (2007-2009)
Minister for Culture, External Affairs and the Constitution (2009)
Cabinet Secretary for Education and Lifelong Learning (2009-2014)

Commissioner-General Malcolm MacDonald with three visiting Dayak chief-tains, 1949. (National Archives of Singapore)

INTRODUCTION

'I saw that island first when it was neither night nor morning. The moon was to the west, setting, but still broad and bright. To the east, and right amidships of the dawn, which was all pink, the daystar sparkled like a diamond. The land breeze blew in our faces, and smelt strong of wild lime and vanilla.'

~ *The Beach at Falesá*, R L Stevenson

THERE ARE MANY REMINDERS in Singapore of the connections with Scotland which date back to the first colonial settlers. A high proportion are clustered inevitably around the oldest part of the city where the early traders would have lived, did business and enjoyed the evening air. None more so than round the rain-browned waters of the Singapore River where one might stand today on the Cavenagh Bridge, turn back to see Anderson Bridge, straining somewhat we can make out through the trees the Dalhousie Obelisk and, dominating the river bank, the imposing structure of the Fullerton Hotel. Looking upstream to the Elgin Bridge, we can glance at the old Parliament House and admire the fine railings protecting the current Singapore Parliament building. On the business side of the river, overshadowed by the leviathans of the commercial world, we can observe the Singapore offices of the Standard Chartered Bank and, turning to Collyer Quay, the Singapore headquarters of the HSBC. We can imagine the vibrancy of Robertson Quay up river just beyond the Elgin Bridge. Each one of these has a strong Scottish connection, name or provenance.

Another cluster is centred around Scotts Road, where once the ordered symmetry of nutmeg plantations and grand houses, approached along elegant driveways, usurped the dense confusion of vibrant tropical growth. Here, Paterson Road, Claymore Hill, Ardmore Park, Anderson Road and Cairnhill Road all bear witness to their Scottish antecedents.

This book tells the story of some of the Scots who helped to develop early Singapore and lay some of the foundations for its undoubted growth and success in later years. Whilst concentrating on the contribution of Scottish administrators, engineers, traders and various professionals, it does not and cannot pretend that no other settlers made a difference.

Cavenagh Bridge and South Boat Quay, c. 1900. (Private Collection)

If it is simplistic to claim that any one person can 'found' a nation; a calumny which is repeated in honorific plaques, busts and statuary from Westminster to Singapore, particularly when the country was clearly in existence for many years before and for some centuries thrived; it is even more inappropriate to suggest that any one national group can claim an exclusive right to the early success of that nation. This book, whilst being deliberately parochial in its concentration, is not designed to detract from the contribution of others. Scots however, were at that time well educated and self reliant, brought up to believe in education and the right of progress to those who applied themselves and had ability. These characteristics were essential in the building of a new settlement.

Many have written histories from a broader perspective and I have drawn heavily on those as source material. All people, most of whom will remain forever unknown, contribute something of value to the development of a nation and its identity.

Scotland at the time of the occupation of Singapore by the English East India Company, was part of the United Kingdom and thereby involved in the creation and development of the British Empire. The disproportionate contribution of Scots to the growth and success of that Empire however, has its roots both in the history of Scotland as an independent nation and its development after the union with England in 1707. Some explanation of the background histories are provided to give a context for Scots leaving their homeland in significant numbers.

An understanding of the Scots character is also relevant and extracts of poetry, song and literature give a flavour of this, although it is also questionable to claim a national characteristic for all its people. To fully understand and appreciate the contribution of the early Scottish founders such as Colonel William Farquhar and Dr John Crawfurd, some of the contextual history of the time is also included.

A significant proportion of the early settlers in Singapore were Scots, of Scottish origins or educated in Scotland. It is this last point that separated Scots from many other peoples in the early 19th century where there was a high degree of literacy and a democratic and meritocratic principle which applied to all. It is not possible to imagine that the overwhelming Scottish majority of early settlers did not leave their mark in Singapore; a majority of the early Residents, a majority of the educators, a majority of the early traders, lawyers and other professionals, were Scottish. Magistrates were drawn from their ranks; early principles of development sprung from their demands as they petitioned Residents for improvements and facilities.

Scottish settlers were also prepared to not only found schools and churches, but pay for them as well in an extension of the principles which they themselves had benefitted from. The concept of the *'lad o' pairts'** has perhaps left some of its legacy in Singapore which is now renowned for its meritocratic policies and high regard for education; these are not new ideas. Those principles of equality so poetically expressed by Robert Burns in his work "A Man's a Man for a' That", are still dearly held.

> Ye see yon birkie ca'd a lord,
> Wha struts, an' stares, an' a' that,
> Tho' hundreds worship at his word,
> He's but a coof for a' that.
> For a' that, an' a' that,
> His ribband, star, an' a' that,
> The man o' independent mind,
> He looks an' laughs at a' that.

The story of early Singapore is one of grand strategy at international level, of exploration, optimism, outrageous egos, personal vendettas, greed and ambition leavened by high principle and missionary zeal of bringing God, education and prosperity to supposedly benighted natives. It is a story of establishing a defendable port, raising it to a settlement and transforming it to a city.

It is a story at many levels, of national ambition, of one company and its desire to make money for its investors; of its employees, who being far from home and with minimal communication from Britain, were largely able to follow their own convictions; and the individuals who followed in its train to take opportunities whether for personal gain or altruism: a story of grandees and landed gentry, military strategists and engineers, sailors and hydrographers, the builders, adventurers and opportunists of every shade, some seeking fame, some fortune and some both.

By the 19th century, the Americas were already significantly developed and the perilous routes to Virginia and the Carolinas were well travelled. The passage to India, the Jewel in the Crown of the British Empire, was also well known by this era. But the valuable trade with China for silks, tea, porcelain and all manner of exotic goods, which had existed on a smaller scale for centuries was, with the development of faster sea travel and greater wealth in

---

Young person with talent, usually from a humble background.

Europe, just beginning to expand. The ambition of the East India Company and that of traders to cash in on the potential would bring Britain ultimately to war with China.

Wars had already been fought to secure a strong foothold in India and frequent skirmishes, battles and sieges would continue to take place. Back in Europe, a century of war with the French was about to draw to a close with the victory at sea at Trafalgar in 1805, and finally on land at Waterloo in 1815. Aggressive competition, resembling often a ritual dance, with the Dutch for the trade in the East Indies and seeking of a port on the long and hazardous journey between China, India and Britain, which had also lasted for a century or more, was nearing its end game.

Singapore in 1819 was an island that had inexplicably been bypassed on many occasions. Its Sanskrit-based name should have alerted interested parties to the possibility that here was once a place of significance and eminence. It had been noted by various mariners in journals and records of their voyages, yet the East India Company and the Dutch had mystifyingly eschewed the location in favour of Malacca, Penang, Rhio, Batavia, Bencoolen and Balambangan and others.

It was a small island, but big enough for a port, to water and victual the ships en route to and from China, a good harbour with freshwater and more importantly, well placed on the sea lanes. As an entrepôt it was ideal, with a ready supply of immigrant labour from India and China. For Europeans, it was hot, humid and sultry, with marshy swamps full of disease, insects and wild animals, and yet with a charming exoticism and an outward appearance of abundance from the lush tropical vegetation and palm-fringed creeks which would beguile them and lure some to linger.

For many, the romance of exoticism would strike them as the South Seas had struck Stevenson. A tropical breeze, the high-pitched whine of insects, a stirring on the creek by fish surfacing to feed, the whirr of colourful tropical birds as they rise up from the deep forest, a myriad of stars in the blackness of sudden nightfall after a spectacular sunset, the heady scent of tropical vegetation and, in those early days, perhaps, the distant, deep throaty growl of a tiger on the prowl.

For many it was a deathtrap. Graveyards would have been one of the first priorities of any settlement. Tropical diseases, harbingers of rapid mortality in a time when there was little understanding of how they were caused, carried or prevented, lent an urgency to all undertakings. Life was short and those from Europe wanted to make money fast and then get home again before it was too late. If Africa's west coast was the white man's graveyard, the East ran a close second.

In the 17th and 18th centuries, a single boatload of pepper, cloves, nutmeg or other spices at the London docks would bring immediate wealth of astounding proportions. By the 19th century, things were not so straightforward but there were still fortunes to be made and positions of importance reached in trading companies which would not be achievable for the majority back home in Scotland.

And where was home? A small country, cold and damp, mountainous with lochs and rivers – the antithesis of Singapore – relentlessly swept alternately by anti-cyclonic weather systems from the Atlantic to the west and icy blasts from the North Sea to the east; one of proud independence and strong culture nurtured for more than 1,000 years. One which prided itself on its education and democratic intellect where education was available to all and an optimism bred from an understanding that where talent existed it would bring success.

But opportunities and outlets for educated people were limited; emigration and travel were in their blood. Scots had travelled to America and India in their droves and, before that, to the Baltic, Eastern Europe and Scandinavia; here was a new opportunity, the East. That opportunity was seized with both hands.

A NEW
ACCOUNT
OF THE
East Indies,

BEING THE
OBSERVATIONS and REMARKS

Of Capt. ALEXANDER HAMILTON,

Who spent his Time there
From the Year 1688. to 1723. Trading
and Travelling, by Sea and Land, to
most of the Countries and Islands of
COMMERCE and NAVIGATION, between the Cape of *Good-hope*, and the
Island of *Japon.*

VOLUME I.

EDINBURGH,
Printed by *John Mosman* One of His MAJE-
STY's Printers, and sold at the King's Prin-
ting-house in *Craig's* Closs. MDCCXXVII.

ONE

The Founding of Singapore

One of the earliest recorded sightings of Singapore was by the Scottish sea captain, privateer and merchant Alexander Hamilton in 1703, where he records in his memoir of voyages:

'In anno 1703 I called at Johor on my way to China and he (the prince of Johor) treated me very kindly and made me a present of the island of Singapore; but I told him that it could be of no use to a private person, though a proper place for a company to settle a colony on, lying in the centre of trade, and accommodated with good rivers and a safe harbour, so conveniently situated that all winds served shipping both to go out and come in to these rivers'.

Some have accused Captain Hamilton of missing a huge opportunity. Bjorn Schelander in his *Singapore: A History of the Lion City*, says, 'had he realised the potential of the area and taken steps to establish a post on the island, Hamilton might have founded a British presence there over one hundred years before Raffles' arrival'.

In fact, 1703 was before the Act of Union when Scotland and England still had their own Parliaments and the United Kingdom of Great Britain did not exist. Hamilton, therefore, could have claimed the land for Scotland. However, the debacle with the Darien Scheme, a catastrophic attempt at colonising part of Central America just about ten years before, had effectively ended Scotland's ability to fund and develop its own colonies; neither did it have any significant naval power to protect it from the Dutch who had a formidable presence in Southeast Asia at that time.

Hamilton was however prescient in pointing out that it would be a good place for a company to settle a colony on. He would be aware, at that time, that the Honourable East India Company was the only organisation, with a monopoly from the English Crown to boot, capable of such an adventure. With so much trade passing nearby, it is astonishing that it had not been considered as a possibility earlier for, as John Keay points out in his *History*

Title page of *A New Account of the East Indies* by Captain Alexander Hamilton.

of the East India Company, 'the name is so impressibly Sanskrit (Singha-Pura – Lion City) that the wonder is that every passing Indophil had not noted the place.'

Arguably the most prominent Scots who had a major influence on the development of Singapore were the administrators, soldiers and officials of the East India Company and then of the British government itself. To fully comprehend the contribution which they made, we should consider at least a little of the history of how and when Singapore was founded and by whom.

It is absurd in many ways to credit anyone with the 'founding' of a place which had, for many thousands of years, passing traders doing regular business as well as occasional kingdoms sited on its sultry shores. However, Europeans love to declare their 'founding' of a place on their first stepping ashore, and the powerful symbolism of planting the flag and claiming territory in the name of the sovereign creates a historical legacy which few, given the opportunity, would eschew.

Natives witnessing such rites would perhaps either stand mystified and mildly amused at the pomp or rush at the invaders with spears, aware, as they would be, that their first gift from Europe was likely to be a sexually transmitted disease. Captain James Cook, another Scot, stepping ashore in Hawai'i, sadly witnessed both options and the gifts of his fellow travellers to the natives were as above described. Thankfully, it appears that the first option was in operation in Singapore, there being some willingness to take advantage of the East India Company's protective firepower and promise of riches, not to say outright bribery.

In spite of the earliest expeditions of the East India Company, set up principally to make money from the spice trade in the 17th century, these forays made little impact because the Dutch had already firmly established themselves and the Company turned its efforts to India. It was only when the trade with China started to increase that the Company had to examine the possibility of a base somewhere on the main sea routes between China and India.

The Company retained an outpost at Bencoolen on the west side of Sumatra, but this was on the wrong side of the main shipping route from the East, the Malacca Strait.

Alternative routes to China were toyed with and opened the possibility of Balambangan on the north Borneo coast being used as a base. However, as J Kennedy in his *History of Malaya* points out, a new base had to ideally to meet three requirements: 'the need for a naval base, the desire to enter the

South-East Asian market, and the need for a port-of-call for English shipping between India and China.'

In 1786, Captain Francis Light proposed Penang to the East India Company, and Sir John MacPherson, a Scot born on the Isle of Skye, Acting Governor-General of India at that time, agreed. Light took possession of Penang later that year, naming it patriotically Prince of Wales Island after the monarch's oldest son and naming the capital Georgetown, after the king himself.

The colony was disorganised from the start, and it was mainly traders

Inset: East India Company coins. (Admiral Nelson Shipwreck Treasure Shoppe, photo copyright: Steven Nelson.) Penang showing Fort Cornwallis, 1810.

and speculators who profited. It wasn't until 1805, the year of British victory at sea against the French at Trafalgar, that the East India Company allocated sufficient funds to run the base adequately. One who arrived in Penang in 1805 was 24-year-old Thomas Stamford Raffles, a newly promoted Assistant Secretary of the EIC, who had served in its London headquarters as a clerk since the age of 14.

Back in Europe, France invaded Holland in 1794/95, a puppet government was installed by the French, and the Dutch King William V fled to England where he made a deal whereby the British were permitted to enter Dutch territories in the East ostensibly to protect them from French incursion. J S Furnivall in his *Netherlands East Indies*, encapsulated the situation succinctly when he said, 'for twenty years from 1795 the unfortunate Dutch had the privilege of being regarded as friends and allies both by France and England; the French overran and ruled their country, and the English took their colonies and their trade'.

It was courtesy of this 'arrangement', known as the Kew Letters, that the British occupied Malacca in 1795 and held it until 1818, just three years after the end of the Napoleonic Wars with the defeat of Napoleon Bonaparte at the Battle of Waterloo.

Malacca was a success under British rule and this caused some friction with Penang which continued to languish. However, presumably because Penang was a British 'possession' and Malacca still only temporarily on loan from the Dutch, the authorities in the East India Company were forced to abandon Malacca and raise the status of Penang.

William Farquhar, an officer of the Madras Engineers of the East India Company, the Resident of Malacca since its takeover by the British, did not agree with this action and protested vehemently and employed various tactics to delay the retreat. He had been asked to demolish the Dutch fortifications and this he resisted vigorously. Finally, using his own judgment and authority, he ordered the preservation of the Dutch church and the Government House or Stadthuys, as well as a number of other public and historic buildings. It is thanks to Farquhar's principles and aesthetic good taste that there is such a rich built heritage remaining in Malacca to this day.

An unlikely ally in the retention and preservation of Malacca turned out to be Raffles who penned a report on the situation and sent a copy to Lord Minto, the Governor-General of India. Gilbert Elliot, the first Earl of Minto, was from a distinguished Scottish family originating in the rural parish of Minto in the Scottish Borders near Hawick. He became a friend and patron

Gilbert Elliot, Earl of Minto.

of Raffles. Raffles's report to the Governor-General, which plagiarized information supplied by Farquhar, proposed the retention of Malacca, pointing out that, 'The land around Malacca was well cultivated, the people were orderly, and they paid their taxes.' An unwitting compliment to Farquhar's effectiveness as Resident.

Minto was a fellow countryman of the talented orientalist and scholar John Leyden*, whom Raffles had befriended and who had put in a good word for Raffles. He was besotted with Raffles's first wife Olivia, a feeling which appeared to have been reciprocated. Leyden's recommendation, Raffles's letter and Farquhar's actions did the trick. Not only was the policy of the directors of the company changed, it also brought Raffles to the attention of Minto, who appointed him as Agent to the Governor-General for the Malay States. In this position, Raffles was asked to organise the invasion of Java and an expedition against the Dutch in 1811.

The invasion of Java under Samuel Auchmuty and Robert Rollo Gilespie was a major and important assault, the French having taken over Java when Holland was annexed. The French General Herman Wiliem Daendels had been appointed Governor and he was making efforts to fortify the Strait between Java and Madura. The British could not allow the French to gain strength and thereby threaten their eastern interests and the lucrative India trade. The invasion involved a total of 324 officers and 11,636 men of which only just over 9,200 were fit for service, the rest being sick, a natural consequence of disease, heat and humidity; an attrition rate close to 25 percent, to

---

*John Leyden was born in 1775 in the town of Denholm in the Scottish Borders close to Lord Minto's estate. He was a talented linguist and orientalist, reputedly having memorised the Bible by the age of eight and later learning 40 languages. Asked if he ever regretted learning any of the many languages he knew, he replied, 'English – it ruined my *guid* (Scots for good) Scots tongue'. Being a countryman, he spoke with a strong accent and, in spite of his many abilities, when he was at university 'his rustic appearance, and strong Teviotdale accent excited a laugh among some of the other students'. This prejudice against his use of the Scots language seems to have been the reason which prevented him from becoming a minister of religion. Yet, Leyden was, as stated by H J Noltie, an embodiment of the 'Enlightenment Scot… (who) typifies the mobility then possible to someone of outstanding ability, by means of the Scottish educational system, and the opportunities presented by the East India Company'. Leyden translated many traditional Malay stories into English but he rarely wrote in Scots. Had he done so, as Scott and Hogg did, he might have been regarded as their equal. He was a significant inspiration to the great writer Sir Walter Scott. John Leyden died in Java in 1811.

John Leyden. (The National Library of Scotland)

Sketch of Dr Leyden taken by Capt ___
on board of the Phoenix on the passage
to Madras in 1811 presented to me by
Dr Leyden in April 1811

This is the handwriting of Colonel McKenzie.

which military commanders had had to become accustomed.

The battle which ensued resulted in the loss of 92 officers and men. The main force landed on 4 August 1811 at the fishing village of Chillinching, eight miles east of Batavia, on the north coast of Java. Meester Cornelis, the main fortress of the Dutch adjacent to Batavia, was stormed and fell to the British invaders on 26 August.

Farquhar was present at the surrender of Soerabaya where he was appointed by Admiral Stopford to the chief civil authority but he did not assume this charge. On his return to Batavia, he was offered the British Residency at Joejakarta, but this he also turned down. On 31 October 1811, Farquhar returned to Malacca.

Lord Minto was also present on board ship at the invasion of Java as, of course, was Raffles. They had been joined by their mutual friend John Leyden. This was to be Leyden's last voyage. Whilst searching for oriental manuscripts and artefacts in Batavia, he contracted a severe fever after entering the foetid atmosphere of a sealed and unaired library. As a result, he died on 28 August 1811 and was buried by Raffles and Minto on Java. The loss was a severe blow to Raffles who relied on Leyden for his knowledge as an orientalist. Minto was also strongly affected by his death.

Sir Walter Scott included a brief eulogy to him in this epic poem on Robert the Bruce:

Quenched is his lamp of varied lore,
That loved the light of song to pour;
A distant and a deadly shore
Has Leyden's cold remains!

The co-commanders of the invasion of Java were Scots. Sir Samuel Auchmuty descended from a family that settled in Fife, Scotland, in the 14th century and had moved to Ireland. Brigadier General Rollo Gillespie was born in County Down, Ireland, but was from an old Scottish family who acquired land in the 18th century and settled in Ireland.

Gillespie's military career reads like a yarn from the *Boys Own Paper*, a weekly periodical published for almost a century replete with tales of Empire and derring-do. His exploits included shooting dead an opponent in a duel and then fleeing to Scotland. He gave himself up and was acquitted after a lengthy trial. His success in taking Batavia from the Dutch was due to his gallantry and good judgement and he was given continued command of the garrison by Auchmuty who left Raffles as civil governor.

During his tenure, Gillespie was involved in a number of local skirmishes which he resolved in characteristic swashbuckling manner. He also had a few skirmishes with Raffles which were not so easily solved and he proferred charges against him in relation to the sale of land and accused him of maladministration, nepotism and corruption.

The East India Company process of enquiry was bureaucratic, Byzantine in its complexity and continued for many years. It was not until after the heroic death of Gillespie – shot through the heart whilst leading his troops against a heavily defended and fortified position in Nepal – that the matter was found mainly in Gillespie's favour. Raffles was acquitted of charges which suggested moral injustice and his character was cleared but judgement was reserved on the wisdom of some of his measures.

The Governor-General of India decided that Raffles's policies in Java were both expensive and imprudent and, at this juncture, Raffles conveniently decided to return to England for health reasons. Whilst there, he wasted no time in courting fame and was lionised by London society and knighted for his book *The History of Java*. He ingratiated himself with landed gentry, including the Duke of Somerset and his Duchess, Lady Charlotte Hamilton, daughter of the Duke of Hamilton, whom he visited in Scotland. Raffles had further connections with Scottish aristocracy through Flora Muire Campbell, Countess of Loudoun, the wife of the Marquis of Hastings, Minto's successor as Governor of India. Lady Hastings was a supporter of Robert Jamieson's Edinburgh University Museum, and it is probable that that connection resulted in botanical specimens from the East being deposited in the Royal Botanical Gardens of Edinburgh and the National Museums of Scotland. Raffles returned to Bencoolen in 1818.

The end of the Napoleonic Wars in 1815 had opened the way for new treaties which resulted in the Dutch possessions, which had been temporarily occupied by Britain, being returned; the Dutch East Indies Company was bankrupt and the Dutch government had taken over their business in the East. The Dutch reemerged more powerful than before. Old treaties were enforced and old animosities resurfaced and were aggravated by Raffles later actions. British ships and traders were once more persona non grata in Dutch possessions.

The East India Company realized, yet again, that the port of Penang was too far north to manage the eastern trade effectively and once more turned their attention to a search for a more southerly port.

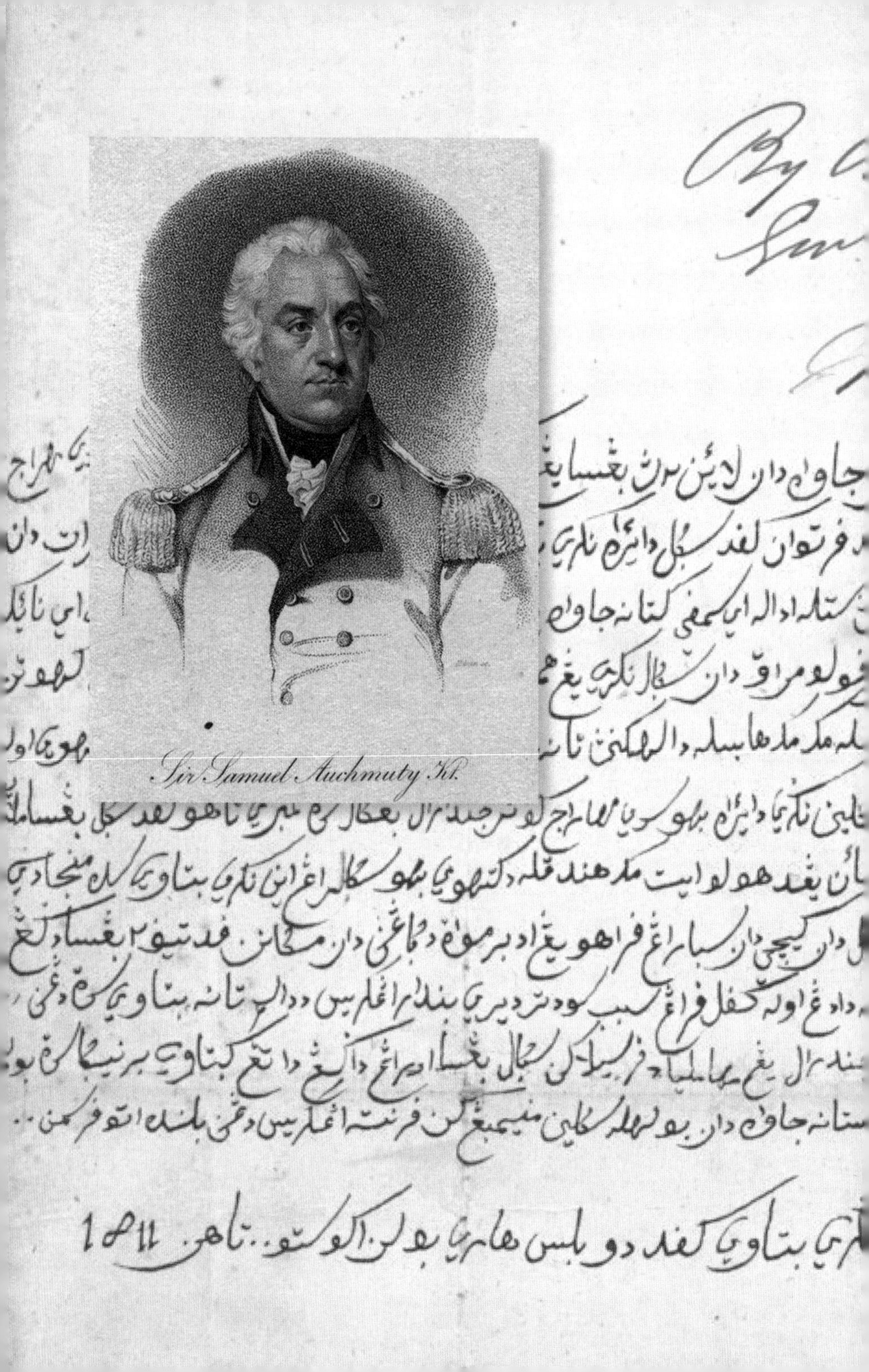
Sir Samuel Auchmuty Kt.

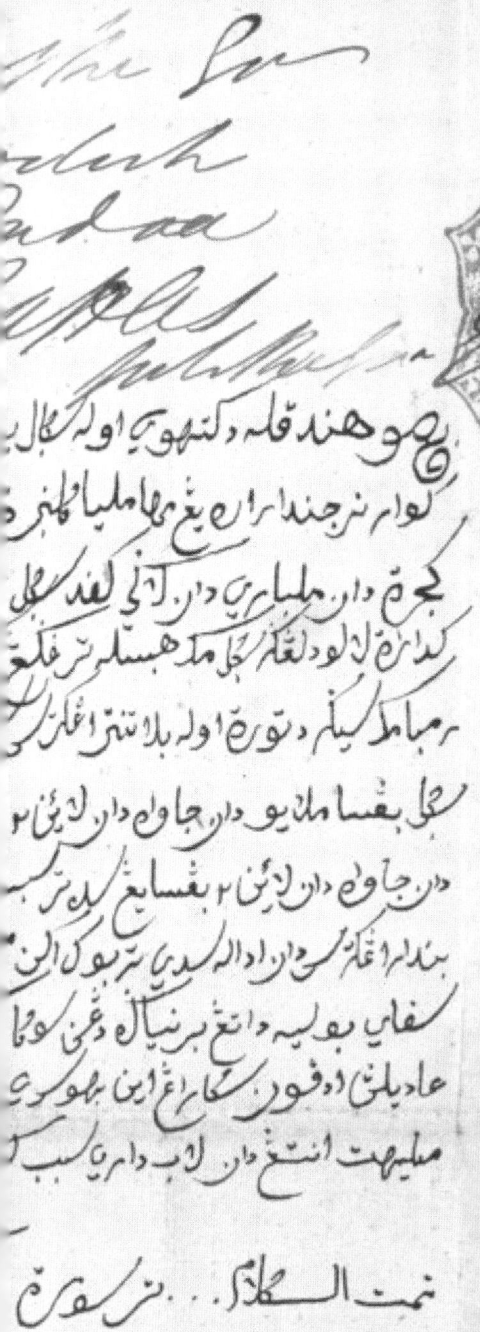

MAJOR-GENERAL WILLIAM FARQUHAR

Early Life

The founding of Singapore is linked inextricably with the story of William Farquhar* who was born in the north east of Scotland at Newhall in the parish of Fetteresso in Kincardineshire near Aberdeen on 26 February 1774. The parish record indicates he was baptised on 19 March in the local church. His father, Robert Farquhar, born in 1723, was a bookseller and landowner. William probably went to a local school in Aberdeenshire, he being one of seven sons. His older brother Arthur had a distinguished career in the Royal Navy and was knighted for his service during the Napoleonic Wars. On retirement from their respective services the two brothers lived in neighbouring properties in Perth.

The outline of Farquhar's military career is documented and listed in Charles Burton Buckley's *Anecdotal History of Old Singapore* originally published by Fraser & Neave in 1902. Buckley's note comes from a record left by Thomas Braddell, an Irishman and the first Attorney-General of the Straits Settlements. There is also information about Farquhar's military career in the very detailed *Military History of the Madras Engineers and Pioneers from June 1743 to the present* by Major H M Vibart.

Military Career

In 1791, at the age of 17, Farquhar was appointed a cadet in the Madras Engineers, one of the many regiments of the East India Company which it used to acquire and protect its interests and enforce trade treaties when necessary.

A few days after arriving in Madras on 19 June 1791, Farquhar was appointed as Ensign, a junior commissioned officer, and in August he joined Lord Charles Cornwallis's Grand Mysore Army.

The following year in 1792, Ensign Farquhar fought at the storming of Nundy Droog[+] under the command of Senior Engineer Lieutenant Mackenzie and two other Ensigns, and at Savern Droog.

These actions, which seem to be minor skirmishes, involved unbelievable hardship and effort with considerable loss of life. It is hard to appreciate from today's perspective the agony of toil, effort and suffering experienced

---

*The name Farquhar derives from Gaelic and the name Fhearchair, meaning 'dear one'.
[+]A *droog* is a steep rocky outcrop which is a distinctive feature of Mysore and Tamil Nadu landscape.

Previous: Sir Samuel Auchmuty (left), Rollo Gillespie (right), proclamation of the capture of Batavia, 1811 (background). Right: Major-General William Farquhar. (Copyright Anna Loake 2010. Reproduced by kind permission of Anna Loake.)

TIPPOO SULTAN.

From an original Picture in the possession of
The Marquis Wellesley

The coming-on of the MONSOONS;—or—The Retreat from SERINGAPATA

Pub.d Dec.r 6th 1791 by H.Humphrey N.o 18 Old Bond Street

"Whats the matter, Falstaff "

by ordinary soldiers of the time. Vibart described part of the action at Nundy Droog: 'the fort is situated on a precipitous granite rock, 2000 feet above the plain. On the easily accessible side, it was defended by two strong walls, and an outwork to cover the gateway'. Several days later he adds, 'elephants were used to drag eight, eighteen pound cannons up the hill'. These were used for bombarding the defences and, some days later, when more ammunition arrived, the breach was made possible and the troops attacked. After the battle, the Senior Engineer, Ensign Farquhar, was commended for his 'skill and indefatigable industry'. Losses during the attack and siege were 120 soldiers.

Ensign Farquhar was also active at the first battle and siege of Seringapatam during the Third Anglo-Mysore war, under the command of Lord Cornwallis with a force of over 20,000 troops drawn from the East India Company and British Army against the ruler of Mysore, Tipu Sultan. Tipu had reportedly 5,000 cavalry and between 40,000 and 50,000 infantry under his command in a heavily defended fortress. Vibart lists the spoils of war and the prize money allocated to the troops after the protracted action in which 535 soldiers were killed or wounded.

The total available for distribution from the three campaigns was 93,584 pounds sterling. The hierarchical division meant that a colonel would have received 1,162 pounds and a private soldier 15 pounds. Farquhar, as an Ensign, would have been given 155 pounds.

In 1793, Farquhar took part in the taking of Pondicherry which had been fought over by the Dutch and French over many decades. In advance of this siege, Ensign Farquhar was appointed as Adjutant of the Engineers. This battle saw the British forces vanquishing the French in part of the wider French revolutionary wars and bringing Pondicherry under British rule until 1814 when it was returned to France. On 16 August 1793, Farquhar was appointed Lieutenant.

Two years after, in July 1795, he became the Chief Engineer to the expedition to Malacca and, in August, he was present at the surrender by the Dutch of Malacca under the terms of the Kew Letters. No battle was engaged and Malacca was transferred to the British without a shot being fired. Farquhar, at this stage, was presumably stationed in Malacca until his recall to Madras on 25 April 1798. His sojourn in Madras was extremely brief, bearing in mind the travel time by ship, before he returned to Malacca at the end of May 1798.

On the first of January 1803, just a month or so short of his 29th birth-

Tipu Sultan, map of the Seige of Serinagapatam, and a cartoon of Lord Cornwallis' hasty retreat from Serinagapatam in 1792.

day, he was promoted to the rank of Captain and rising ever more rapidly, succeeded Colonel Taylor in civil and military authority in Malacca on 12 July 1803.

Seven years later on 25 June 1810, he gained further promotion to Brevet Major and on 26 September 1811, he was given the full rank of Corps Major and appointed by the commander Sir Samuel Auchmuty to be in charge of intelligence and guides in the forthcoming expedition to Java.

Farquhar's progress through the ranks was sure and steady, not a meteoric rise but nevertheless rapid. Each time, there was clear purpose to the progress – not merely a time server – and he must have proved himself with some distinction to be marked out, in particular, to take over from Colonel Taylor at Malacca at the age of 37, and for the later more advanced promotions and finally to be noticed by the commander of the army and selected for a key role in the important military adventure to invade the island of Java in 1811.

Farquhar's distinguished military record is as follows: Cadet 1791, Ensign 10 July 1791, Lieutenant 11 August 1793, Captain 1 Jan 1803, Major 26 September 1811, Lieutenant Colonel 9 May 1821, Colonel-Commandant 8 September 1824, and Colonel 5 June 1829.

His promotion to Major General came on retirement from service in January 1837.

Resident of Malacca

William Farquhar acted as Resident of Malacca from 1803. In December 1813, he was appointed as Resident and Commandant of Malacca, a position which he held until the port was returned to the Dutch by agreement in 1818.

Munshi Abdullah, the Malaccan-born Malay writer, described Farquhar in his *Hakayat Abdullah* as 'a man of good parts, slow at fault finding, treating rich and poor alike, and very patient in listening to the complaints of any person who went to him, so that all returned rejoicing'.

Farquhar's residency in Malacca was marked by successful and steady progress and there appears to have been no demand, as there had been earlier, for a search for a more suitable port to meet the needs of the East India Company's expanding China trade. It was not until 1818, when the reality of having to cede the territory back to the Dutch hit them, that the Company awoke to the issue. J Kennedy, in his *A History of Malaya*, pointed out that Farquhar's last actions as Resident in Malacca were far from petulant and

View of Malacca from the Straits.

self-serving as they might have been but forward looking and strategic. He recorded: 'during his last months at Malacca Farquhar had not been idle in promoting the interests of his Company. He had made treaties allowing company trade with Malay rulers at Siak in Sumatra, and Rhio and Lingga in the Archipelago; he also had ideas about the possibility of a British Settlement in the Carimon islands'.

The final acceptance that Penang was too far from the main shipping lanes was, not surprisingly, upsetting to the Governor of Penang, John Bannerman, a Scot and son of the manse, from Perth, who, in trying to defend his interests in maintaining the more northerly port, became obstructive.

Bannerman, in not the first of a series of personality clashes, was scarcely a fan of Raffles. Born in 1759, Bannerman joined the Madras Regiment like Farquhar as a cadet at the age of 17 and sailed to India shortly afterwards. He progressed through the ranks and became Lieutenant Colonel in 1800 and, after retiring from the regiment in 1803, became a director of the East India Company in 1808 and was appointed Governor of Penang in 1816. A

seasoned soldier, investor, company man and diplomat, it is unlikely Bannerman would have done anything which might damage the company to which he had devoted, and no doubt frequently risked his life. He thought Raffles's methods were irreverent, dangerous and a threat to the stability of the East India Company.

Raffles, even when he was safely out of the way in relatively remote Bencoolen, was active in trying to promote British interests in Sumatra. Not surprisingly, this annoyed the Dutch but also the British as they were complicit in the rebuilding of Dutch influence as a counterweight to ensure that the French never again reached a position of strength following the end of the recent protracted wars. Kennedy stated that 'Raffles was censured by the Company for his conduct'.

A New Port

The direction for a return to the search for a port came not from the inspiration of those in the area but direct from Calcutta where Warren Hastings, the Governor-General of India, issued instructions to Raffles and commanded him to seek out a suitable port in Rhio* and, if that was no longer available, to consider Johore. At this point, Hastings, Farquhar and Raffles seem to be of the same view that Rhio was the best option for a southerly base, but by the time they realised this and did anything about it, it was too late. The Dutch strength was growing and Rhio, as would soon be discovered, had been well and truly occupied and recommissioned by them. It is astonishing that whilst the Dutch were in irons that more effort was not made to take advantage and secure a more southerly port.

Raffles set sail from Calcutta in December of 1818 and headed to Penang where he joined Farquhar who was to accompany him on the search for the elusive southern port. Farquhar had been due for home leave back in Britain after his successful handover of Malacca to the Dutch. However, Hastings, demonstrating considerable optimism and a positive approach, as well as obvious faith in Farquhar, had nominated him to be the Resident of the new settlement wherever it turned out to be. Raffles, in the meantime, remained the Lieutenant Governor of Bencoolen. Having said that, Farquhar was to operate under Raffles instruction for the quest.

The small flotilla sailed from Penang on 18 January without Raffles who was held up by a dispute with Bannerman. Raffles therefore followed

---

*Riau Islands, now part of Indonesia.

Farquhar in a separate ship, catching up with him at the Carimoon Islands, an archipelago now in Indonesia, on 27 January 1819.

The Carimoons were found to be unsuitable as it was confirmed that Rhio had indeed been fully occupied by the Dutch. It was then when Captain Daniel Ross of the ship *Discovery* and hydrographer of the Company's private navy Bombay Marine, suggested taking a look at Singapore. Seven ships set sail and arrived at Singapore on 28 January at 4 pm.

John Keay, in his *History of the East India Company*, reminded us in relation to the selection of the port that, 'it is not certain that the idea was his, (Raffles). Farquhar had certainly suggested Singapore; so had Captain Ross'. Of Raffles, Keay pointed out, 'Fame he craved more than fortune'.

Ross's suggestion is often overlooked and is mentioned only in a passing whisper so as not to draw attention from the self-aggrandising Raffles, but Ross was no slouch. He was engaged, at the time of this attachment, on a survey in the area. He was a distinguished hydrographer, Master Attendant at Bombay and President of the Bombay Geographical Society. His reputation was second only to that of James Horsburgh, the eminent hydrographer, and was known as 'Father of the Indian Surveys'. He was also highly regarded for his surveys of the China Seas which he undertook from 1806 to 1820, so he was more than familiar with the area.

Details of his birth are sparse, but Ross is a Scottish name and it appears that he might have been born in Jamaica to the muscularly named Hercules Ross, an emigree Scot with a colourful life, most of whose 13 children were born in Scotland. Hercules returned to Scotland in the 1760s and bought the Rossie Estate. Captain Ross had a half brother, also Daniel, who reputedly was hung from the yardarm by Nelson as a privateer. Captain Ross died in Bombay shortly after his retirement in 1849.

Farquhar and Raffles landed on the next day, 29 January 1819, although some contemporary accounts suggest that Farquhar was alone on the first landing; and on that day negotiated and signed a temporary agreement for the East India Company to set up what the East India Company termed a 'factory', in other words a port facility for trading purposes. A further agreement was signed on 6 February in return for protection and $5,000 a year for the Sultan and $3,000 a year for the Temenggong.

Raffles then left Farquhar with some instructions on how to organise the new port and left for Acheh and Bencoolen the next day. It is often asserted that Raffles landed on the island, planted the British flag and proclaimed the territory for Britain. This is an exaggeration of the position as only a small

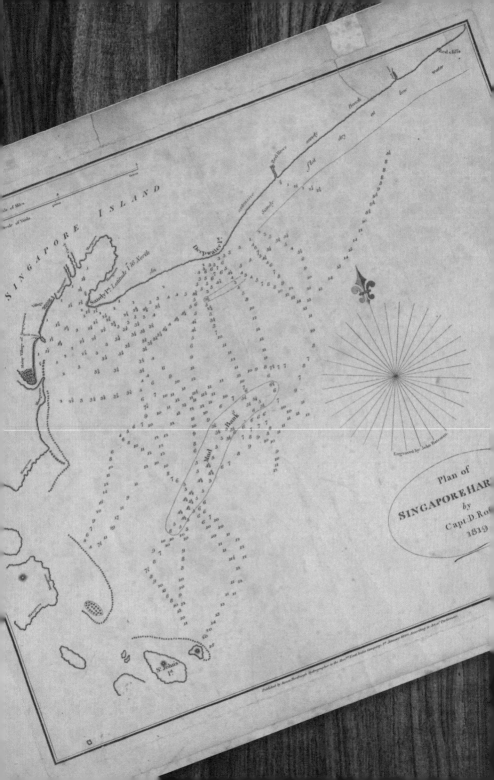

Plan of
SINGAPORE HAR
by
Capt. D. Ro
1819

portion of land around the port was subject to the treaty, no sovereignty over the native population was transferred, no permanent cession of territory was agreed, nor was the deal made on behalf of the United Kingdom. Rather, it was for the Honourable East India Company for the purpose of, they hoped, profitable exercise of their trading monopoly.

Success was far from guaranteed. Many attempts had been made in other ports in parts of Southeast Asia by various nations; most had faded into insignificance. The port had yet to be accepted by the East India Company where opinion was divided. Creating favourable conditions for traders in a completely new and untested port was a high-risk strategy, not to mention the possibility of a major attack from the Dutch who, when they found out, would be thoroughly upset at the prospect of a British trading post close to their doorstep.

The opinion of Horsburgh was highly respected and no doubt carried some weight to help sway the minds of the East India Company Directors to retain the new settlement. In 1819, he wrote in a paper to the Court of Directors: 'the Straits of Sunda and Malacca are the two gates or barriers leading into the China Sea for all the commerce of British India, Europe and the Eastern coasts of North and South America, which gates the Dutch fully command, if we do not retain the settlement at Singapore'. Horsburgh added, 'If we retain the settlement of Singapore, great security will be afforded to our China trade in the event of war.'

As expected, when the Dutch did discover the annexation of land for the 'factory', they demanded immediate withdrawal and threatened action. Neither Britain nor the East India Company were impressed by Raffles's activities, thinking that he had overstepped the mark and exceeded orders. However, neither did the British want to appear weak by withdrawing, so they waited to see who would blink first. Bannerman in Penang was asked to send some soldiers for protection of the settlement, but this proved to be unnecessarily pessimistic as no invasion came from the Dutch who engaged in nothing more bellicose than further sabre rattling. In the meantime, under the steady and sympathetic guidance and leadership of Farquhar, the new port quickly became established and grew rapidly. The population grew. East Indiamen en route to and from China used the port and shared the harbour with junks and other vessels as the trade with China expanded.

On 14 October 1820, Captain Archibald Hamilton, writing to British statesman Robert Dundas, Lord Melville, confirmed his opinion that Farquhar was the right man for the job in Singapore: 'the fortunate selection

Plan Of Singapore Harbour By Captain D Ross, 1820. (Survey Department, Singapore; National Archives of Singapore)

of Colonel Farquhar as the settler, a man of the most mild and conciliatory character with all, who had resided for the last 25 years at Malacca, 17 or 19 of which he was Governor, and who is beloved by all classes of the inhabitants, is of itself a circumstance of the most fortuitous nature for this infant settlement'.

By 1820, the revenues of the port were meeting the cost of administration and, within three years of its founding, in 1822, it had overtaken the trade of Penang, a port which had been in use since 1786 when Francis Light first stepped ashore.

Ernest C T Chew, in his essay 'The Foundation of a British Settlement' in *A History of Singapore*, points out that, 'certainly it was Farquhar who worked alongside the Malay authorities for the next four years to secure the survival and growth of the British Settlement on Singapore Island'. Chew continued, 'If he, (Raffles), is to be honoured as the founder and architect of the British 'factory' in Singapore, then the early and enterprising builders (who modified his designs), should also be commemorated: the first two British Residents, Farquhar, (1819-23) and John Crawfurd, (1823-26), along with the known Malay, Bugis, Chinese, Indian and European notable, (mostly traders), and the numberless, unnamed pioneering settlers'.

Many of those 'unnamed settlers' were Scots, as were most of the traders. The population statistics of the early days of the settlement are speculative but the Reverend George Murray Reith, a Scottish minister, in his *Handbook to Singapore 1892*, stated that, in 1819, the population was about 200 with no more than 50 of these being Chinaman. He adds that by 1822 the population was 10,000. In light of later, more accurate figures, these estimates look reasonable and neither Farquhar, nor indeed anyone else, had any precedent for dealing with such rapid growth and increase in activity in the new settlement of Singapore.

The port activity was of paramount importance and, as early as September 1819, Farquhar advocated the use and advantages of the present day Keppel Harbour area as the town developed around the Singapore River. It was Farquhar's initiative which got the new harbour established and Dr Carl A Gibson-Hill in *Memoir of the Raffles Museum No. 3*, December 1956, suggested that, 'it would have been fairer to have called it Farquhar's Harbour'.

The Need for Land
The land around the harbour area near the river was covered on one side by low jungle and, with a small population, the island would have been teeming

Top: **Proposed plan of Singapore town by Lieut Philip Jackson (Survey Department, Singapore; National Archives of Singapore). Bottom: Lieut Philip Jackson's sketch of Singapore, 1823.**

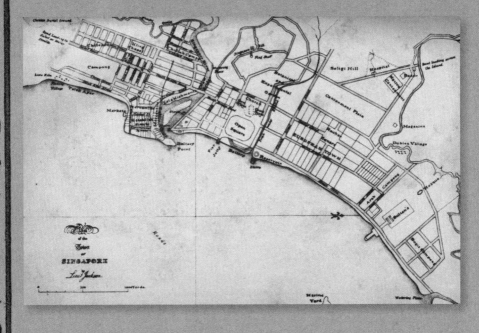

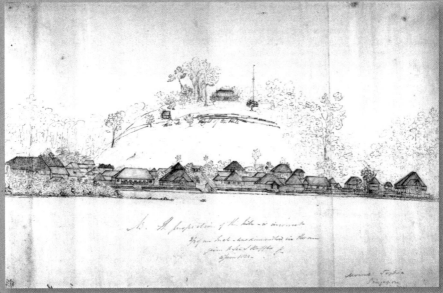

with birds and wildlife of all descriptions. Farquhar, we are told by Buckley, was the first European to ascend the hill, Bukit Larangan, now Fort Canning, reputedly the burial place of old Rajahs. A gun was also taken up and a salute fired from the summit. Orders were given by Farquhar to clear the hill and Government House was afterwards constructed on the site. Farquhar also arranged for angsana trees to be transported from Malacca and planted in the area of the Esplanade.

Early work in the new colony for which the Resident was responsible included setting up watering arrangements for shipping, clearing land for building, establishing a system for allocating building plots, filling up swamps, creating a road network, making bridges across rivers and planting of trees. Spice plants were planted on Government Hill and nutmeg trees planted in various locations close by.

According to Buckley, quoting Abdullah, Farquhar went for a walk each morning to review the land available and found it mostly thick with jungle, mangroves and trees with only one good part in the centre. 'There was not a spot of good land, except a place ten fathoms wide, the rest was a mud flat except the hills. There was a large hill at the mouth of the Singapore River.'

The work of the Resident would have to cover everything related to the founding, maintenance and development of a new settlement. Defensive bastions for cannon, magazines for storing the shot, cannonball and explosives, roads, bridges, ensuring water was available, developing the harbour, all were the priority for Farquhar. If any question arose, the turn-around time for a letter from Bencoolen, subject as it was to the availability of sailing vessels and the vagaries of wind and tide, would take many weeks by which time it would be too late.

Decisions had to be made on the spot and Farquhar was used to doing that from his experience in Malacca and in the army.

Farquhar was involved frequently in a number of discussions and disputes relating to the harbour and allocation of land. Some residents still considered the harbour too small and it was again suggested that the Carimoon Islands would be more suitable. Farquhar reviewed this but presumably decided against taking any action. He, also at this time, decided to allocate some farms for opium, arrack and gambling activity. This again was one of the bones of contention when Raffles finally dispensed with Farquhar's services in 1823. But the money that these raised was necessary for the development of facilities.

Shortage of land, then as now, was causing problems. Farquhar wrote to

Raffles: '...nothing is heard in the shape of complaint but the want of more ground to build upon'. Not surprisingly, the allocation of land became an issue. Swampy ground had to be avoided or else filled in in some way. It was agreed that the swamp on the north bank of the river would be filled in by excavating a nearby hill to build Boat Quay.

Raffles's plan had been to reserve land north of the river for government buildings and use the next parcel of land up to the Rochor River for building by the merchants. The merchants pointed out to Farquhar that it would be more convenient if they could be next to the river. Farquhar reserved land from north beach to the stream at Bras Basah and thus preserved what became the esplanade area. It is thanks to Farquhar's efforts that this area was retained for recreational purposes which remains to this day.

Developing the New Settlement
Buckley provided information on the number of vessels coming in to the Singapore harbor in 1822. There were, we are told, 139 square riggers and 1,434 native craft. This rise of commerce was due, Buckley added, to the principle of free trade on which Singapore was founded. It is to the credit of Resident Farquhar that this principle was upheld in the early days of the port.

Singapore was a success. In spite of Raffles's much vaunted reports on the possibility of Java being as lucrative a venture as India to the East India Company, he failed to notice that, whilst 'this other India' rich in produce and history and, he claimed, the greatest commercial asset in the archipelago, the East India Company was not interested in the retention of Java and what is more, his controversial reforms during his tenure as Governor did not produce any surplus.

Keay also reminded us that Raffles was not known for his free-trade principles. He championed in Java, 'the extension of our liberal and national principles of monopoly' in relation to the spice trade, to the opium trade and to the import of Indian cottons. Similarly, at Bencoolen, Sumatra, he promoted a colonisation and plantation economy in which the company would remain as the purchasing agency.

Keay stated that it was not Raffles's idea, but that of Alexander Dalrymple, the East India Company's first hydrographer, born into a distinguished Edinburgh family in 1737, who had proposed a free port at Balambangan as early as 1763. This was effectively an anticipation of the principles which, together with the example of Penang where for the first decade or so no duties

Lines of Singapore

Old Lines of Singapore

Flag-Staff

Fresh Battery

Parade

Ferry point

Rocky point

Kampong China

2

Singapore from the Rocky Point 1819

Left: Map of Singapore showing Rocky Point where the Singapore Stone was found, 1825. Top: Sketch of Singapore, 1819 (Courtesy of the National Museum of Singapore, National Heritage Board). Bottom: Drawing of a fragment of the Singapore Stone.

had been charged, inspired Singapore's free port status. Dalrymple, as a Scot, would have been familiar with the free market principles espoused by Adam Smith, the political economist born across the water from Edinburgh in Fife.

Writing in 1834, Captain Peter James Begbie of the Madras Artillery, an Edinburgh man born in 1804, in his book, *The Malay Peninsula*, paints a lyrical and poetic picture of the still new settlement: 'the harbour presents a bustling and pleasing scene. Outside of the merchantmen are the King's ships, easily to be distinguished by their long, low, hulls, whilst their light and fairy masts and spars rest in faint and delicate relief against the deep blue sky; next to them, the huge Indiamen are to be seen, like Leviathans half emerging from the deep'. His comment extends to the landward side as well, he continues, 'The houses are generally good and the streets regular and clean. The whole town has an appearance of great bustle and activity'.

Begbie also attempts to shed some light on the mystery of the Singapore stone which was sadly substantially destroyed. Etched with a so-far untranslated inscription, it was found near the mouth of the Singapore River, and a fragment is now housed in the National Museum of Singapore. He refers to the *Malay Annals* translated and recorded by John Leyden and records some of the interesting legends which might have had a bearing on the provenance of the stone.

Begbie was promoted to Major-General on his retirement, recorded in *The Edinburgh Gazette*, 5 February 1858. He died in 1864.

Begbie's description provides an independent comment on not only the commercial success of the port but the general demeanour and appearance, all of which derive not from written pronouncements made from afar but from practical action.

Local Tradition

In October 1822 in Singapore, 50 slaves were imported and sold. Raffles reminded the Resident that this was against British law but Farquhar replied that he had allowed it as it was a local tradition. This does seem to be a weak moral stance to take and, unsurprisingly, Raffles used this episode in making his final decision to dismiss Farquhar the following year.

Farquhar was noted for his empathy with local people, their dress and traditions, a less arrogant stance than many colonial administrators might take. However, the acceptance of local culture cannot transcend and excuse the turning of a blind eye to basic human right.

Living with a local woman and enjoying local life, it was well known that Farquhar also dressed in a sarong like the locals. Although he did not completely 'go native', he was a Malay speaker and had made some effort to understand Malay culture and society, doing his best to fit in with the local people. Farquhar must have blended well with the local population in Malacca where he was known as the Rajah of Malacca. This affinity with local customs and families, which no doubt continued once he had assumed the Residency of Singapore, was yet another reason for his falling out with Raffles and Raffles's brother-in-law, Master Attendant William Flint, who smouldered with self-righteous and were clearly affronted by what they saw as a fall from grace from not upholding the standards expected of a *sahib*.

In a climate such as Singapore's, wearing of European dress, consisting of neck-bruising high collars, breath-choking cravats or neckcloths wound round the throat, tailcoats, tight breeches and silk stockings, would have been stifling and exhausting. The adoption of 'native dress' would have been a welcome relief to Europeans literally bound in their own native garb without the benefit of lightweight modern materials.

Contemporary portraits of Farquhar depict him in military uniform. A handsome man standing stiffly in a high collared scarlet tunic with gold epaulettes and braiding to the front. He sports a mop of luxuriant grey hair, balding on top. He stares out with an avuncular yet authoritative gaze. It is not the manner of dress one could wear in comfort in Singapore for any length of time. Raffles, in contrast with the military bearing of Farquhar, takes the pose of a dandy. His portraits describe a romantic, slightly effete man with full lips, a full head of slightly unruly hair with very long sideburns as was the fashion of the time. His statue on the bank of the Singapore River depicts him in the high collar of the times under a single-breasted tailcoat, tight knee breeches and stockings, looking imperiously down at all passers by.

Public Order

The population of Singapore continued to grow and we are told by Buckley that there were regular disturbances between the Malacca Malays, the Chinese and the Klings*, he adds, 'had they not been afraid of Mr Farquhar there would have been murder among them every day.'

But there was murder in the new colony, one of the intended victims being Colonel Farquhar himself. On 11 March 1823, Farquhar was stabbed by an Arab named Syed Yassin who had run amok. Yassin, a trader from

---

*At the time, a general term for Indians.

Pahang, had purchased goods from one Syed Omar but did not have the money to pay for them. Farquhar, in an earlier hearing, had given judgement in Omar's favour, so it was pay up or go to jail.

Yassin clearly did not want to go to jail and as he was dragged off pleaded to speak to Omar and make an arrangement to delay settlement of the debt. On the approach to Omar's house the peon guarding him suspected his intentions; Yassin, who had a kris concealed in his cloak, whipped it out, killed the peon on the spot and rushed off.

Farquhar was called and courageously went out to search armed only with a stick. Yassin was hiding under Omar's house and when Farquhar was poking about, Yassin leapt out and stabbed him in the chest. Sepoys were called and Yassin was quickly apprehended and run through.

Farquhar had sustained a serious though not life threatening injury, and was quickly cleaned and bandaged by Dr William Montgomerie, the Assistant Surgeon. Raffles being in Singapore at that time, decided to make an example of Yassin by parading his remains round the town in a cart, accompanied by a beating gong to draw attention to the fate of miscreants, prior to being encaged and left to rot at Telok Ayer point for a fortnight.

An extreme reaction perhaps, but there were but a handful of Europeans in the midst of 10,000 Malay, Chinese and other natives and, if control there must be, fear had to be one of the most effective means in the absence of a dedicated police force. Such actions are however, just as morally reprehensible as turning a blind eye to slavery. Raffles and Farquhar were both products of their era and subject to the mores of their times and neither one can claim moral superiority over the other in spite of Raffles's later moralist rhetoric on his dismissal of Farquhar.

Dispute and Dismissal

Raffles himself clearly had a good opinion of Farquhar in the early stages of the settlement. On 8 June 1819, Raffles wrote to Hastings, the Governor General of India, 'The exertions of Major Farquhar during my short absence have been indefatigable – the country has assumed a new appearance, the harbour is filled with shipping and our defences are already very respectable'.

Raffles's opinion changed however, and in the final year of Farquhar's Residency he wrote to the East India Company and commented on his belief that Farquhar was not up to the job. He pointed out that he may have done well so far but he considered him unequal to the task now that Singapore had reached a position of eminence. Raffles referred to weaknesses of

Singapore from the Gov.l Bungalow Nov 14.th 1828.

favouritism and irregularities, none of which have been substantiated. We have seen that Raffles himself was not immune to weakness and, as far as favouritism goes, he was quick to appoint his own relatives to positions of influence and authority.

There was no shortage of nepotism in the East India Company and we hear that Farquhar appointed his own son-in-law, Mr Francis James Bernard, as his assistant as well as Master Attendant until the arrival of Captain Flint, the brother-in-law of Stamford Raffles, who then assumed the latter post. This transfer of authority for an important position seems to be at the root of the animosity which coloured the relationship between Flint and Farquhar. In turn, Flint, no doubt having the ear of Raffles, probably used every opportunity to undermine the position of the Resident and was instrumental in Farquhar's dismissal.

Raffles's previous record as a mere clerk for 10 years in the London offices of the East India Company and his questionable management of Bencoo-

Singapore habour from the government bungalow on Fort Canning Hill, 1828. (Courtesy of the National Museum of Singapore, National Heritage Board)

len and Java does not support his claim as being the designer of the success of Singapore. For that part, it needed a man of proven worth, an engineer, a soldier of acknowledged courage, skill and experience and an able administrator with long experience in Malacca which had been a success under its relatively brief British rule; in other words: Major Farquhar.

Farquhar ensured the defence of the new colony of Singapore which, as a soldier and engineer, he was well qualified to undertake, and was active in seeking out the best harbour. With little or no funds allocated to him by the East India Company, it is recorded that he used his own money to pay for clerks.

When Major Farquhar left Singapore in December 1823, he was presented at a farewell dinner with a silver epergne by the traders and residents of Singapore. Farquhar's popularity was referred to by Abdullah, in his *Hikayat Abdullah*, who recalls that on the day of Farquhar's departure he was accompanied to the beach by most of the European inhabitants of the settlement as well as by a 'large concourse' of Asians of every class. Troops formed a guard of honour from his house to the departing craft and many boats accompanied him out to the ship *Alexander*. A number of tribute salutes were fired and similar salutes were fired as his vessel progressed up the Strait to Malacca and Penang.

On his arrival back in Britain, Farquhar petitioned the East India Company about the unreasonable treatment he received from Raffles, which many agree was shabby at best. Raffles was economical with the truth in his statements in defence to the Board of Directors and the Board took no action on Farquhar's request to be recognised as one of the founders of Singapore. Farquhar's case was not helped by the fact that the Assistant Secretary of the Company was Raffles's brother-in-law.

Farquhar's dismissal was never fully justified. The reasons given by Raffles are inconsequential given the standards of the time and we are left to draw our own conclusions on the motives for Raffles's intemperate action. Singapore was a success and had Farquhar continued in post as Resident, it is likely that his name would have become more associated with the city than that of Raffles. This Raffles could not risk. In a determination to secure his place in history, he sought to blacken the name of William Farquhar and ensure that no one was in a position to dispute his claim to being the sole founder of Singapore.

In spite of the formal rebuff from the Court of Directors, two of its members hosted a formal dinner of thanks for Farquhar to which a great many

The silver epergne presented to William Farquhar at his departure from Singapore. (Courtesy of the National Museum of Singapore, National Heritage Board)

friends and colleagues were invited and where many toasts were drunk and generous expressions of regard for Farquhar espoused.

Natural History

Buckley records that whilst Farquhar was walking one morning by the Rochor River, one of his dogs was taken by an alligator which was then surrounded and killed. 'It was eighteen feet long and its body was hung on the banyan tree at Bras Basah.' No mention was made of the fate of the dog which presumably did not survive the attack. Alligators were clearly common in Singapore then. In 1862, John Thomson, the photographer from Edinburgh, visited Mr Rarey, magistrate, and found him stuffing such a reptile which was, perhaps more realistically, 12 feet long.

Thomson described the scene: 'There stretched out upon tressles, and with its capacious full-fanged jaws at their widest, lay the largest alligator I had ever seen. I am stuffing this monster, said Rarey, and shall send it to my brother to set up in his hall; for he, like myself, is fond of curiosities which cannot be picked up every day. He has been a man-eater, this fellow, no mistake about it; but there's no stuffing the brute. I wish one or two of my peons (native servant), would crawl down his throat. They would never be missed.'

Further encounters with wildlife, reported by Buckley, included that in response to a plague of rats. The enterprising Major did not pipe them out of the city but offered a bounty of one anna for each dead rat delivered to the Resident. The incentive was immediately effective and quickly disposed of the offending rodents. In an echo of Biblical plagues, this was followed by great number of stinging centipedes; no doubt a tasty component of the diet of the rat; for which a small reward was also offered and the nuisance thus eliminated.

Alfred Russel Wallace, the distinguished naturalist who, during his research and travels in the East, explored the principles of natural selection and evolution and can be credited equally with Charles Darwin for his discoveries, wrote of his visits to Singapore between 1854 and 1862 in *The Malay Archipelago*. He commented on the number of tigers still roaming freely: 'There are always a few tigers roaming about Singapore, and they kill on average a Chinamen every day, principally those who work in gambir plantations, which are always made in newly cleared jungle. We heard a tiger roar once or twice in the evening, and it was rather nervous work hunting for insects among the fallen trunks and old sawpits when one of those savage animals might be lurking close by, waiting an opportunity to spring upon us'.

Wallace himself, although born in Wales, claimed a Scottish origin. He stated in his own memoir, *My Life – a Record of Events and Opinions* published in 1905, that his family was descended from the Scottish freedom fighter William Wallace. He cited as evidence that his family crest shared the device of an ostrich with a horseshoe in its mouth with the crest of the Craigie-Wallace family who were known to be descendants of the patriot.

Though not a professional naturalist like Wallace, Farquhar, in addition to being a competent administrator, gallant soldier and competent engineer, had a keen interest in the natural world. Growing up in Aberdeenshire, he was close to the Cairngorm mountains which had abundant wildlife of red deer and wildcat. Salmon and trout were plentiful in the region's famed rivers the Don, the Dee and the Spey, and the skies above the high tops would have been graced by the flight of eagles and buzzard with grouse and ptarmigan bursting noisily from the heather when disturbed.

His military career in India, with its ever present dangers, would have opened his eyes to a different style of life but without much time in a busy schedule to relax and contemplate what he was seeing and experiencing. However, when he got to Malacca, his time was not so constrained and he was able to appreciate the languid surroundings of creeks, warm seas and tropical forests. His keen interest in nature prompted him to gather specimens of many species of plants and animals. He commissioned men to go to the forests, rivers and seas to collect specimens and unusually, commission Chinese artists to paint them to make a permanent record of the variety of creatures and plants.

The paintings Farquhar commissioned are vibrant with colour and anatomically and botanically accurate, leaving us with a unique combination of art and science and a record of unparalleled beauty and interest. Farquhar's Collection is of considerable importance and spans his years in Malacca from 1803 to 1818. The collection was presented by him to the Royal Asiatic Society in 1827 who sold it in its entirety in 1995. It was purchased by Mr Goh Geok Khim of Singapore and generously gifted by him to the National Museum of Singapore where it remains on permanent display as a memorial to the man who did so much to establish and develop early Singapore.

In a review in the *Financial Times*, 4 January 2013, Harry Eyres commented on his favourite work: "I especially like the Malayan Tapir, a species Farquhar discovered and a specimen of which he kept as a pet. He praised its 'mild and gentle disposition', (maybe not so different from his own) and sympathetically noted that 'it seemed very susceptible of cold'."

Overleaf, clockwise from left: Tapir, Pied Triller and Durian, Pepper Plant, and Wild Jasmine from the William Farquhar Collection of Natural History Drawings. (By courtesy of Mr G K Goh)

Tapir of Malacca

Durio zibethinus

Deorian. Boorang Brush Bloss?ry بوریغ بکرس — فوکۃ دریان

Raffles was also interested in natural history but it is clear that Farquhar was the master and Raffles the pupil. Raffles learned a lot from Farquhar and as H J Noltie states in the book, *Raffles Ark Redrawn*, 'Raffles failed to pay adequate credit to Farquhar's influence in several different areas, one of which is Farquhar's role as a mentor in natural history studies and its documentation through art'. It is likely that Raffles was strongly influenced by Farquhar's extensive and stunning collection of works as well as by his methods of preserving and recording.

Raffles also became a collector of specimens of flora and fauna and, besides being tutored by Farquhar, he was influenced and aided by two other Scots in this field. One was John Leyden, the multi-skilled and talented scholar, orientalist and linguist who was also trained as a doctor and naturalist. Leyden stayed three months with Raffles in Penang in 1805-06 and later accompanied him on the invasion of Java. The other was Dr Joseph Arnold, trained at the Edinburgh Medical School and an East India Company surgeon. On return from a voyage delivering convicts to Botany Bay, he was stranded on the return journey for three months in 1818 in Java where he befriended Raffles and undertook work collecting specimens of the natural world. *Rafflesia arnoldii*, the world's largest flowering plant, discovered by Arnold's Indonesian guide, is named in Arnold's honour.

H J Noltie further elaborates Raffles's connections with Scotland with the revelation that not only was the the Raffles Collection held in Inshriach House, Scotland, from 1939 to 1969 but that 'one of the more extraordinary discoveries was that 24 of the botanical drawings of the Raffles Collection, were, in fact, made for William Hunter, a Scottish East India Company surgeon, by a Chinese artist in Penang, in the three years prior to Raffles' arrival there, and most probably acquired by him following Hunter's death in Java in 1812.'

Farquhar in fact made several discoveries, to Westerners at least, that were new to science both in botany and zoology; included amongst these were the Malayan Tapir, the bearcat, (a civet-like creature,) and the banded linsang, (a tree-dwelling carnivorous mammal also similar to a civet); none of these mammals bears the name of their 'discoverer'. Raffles was at the very least ungracious in reporting these discoveries and others without any acknowledgement of Farquhar's contribution. Raffles's silence over this echoes his earlier reluctance to acknowledge Farquhar's vital contribution on two previous occasions, firstly the gathering of intelligence for the report to Hastings on the position in Malacca prior to its return to the Dutch and

Joseph Arnold.

secondly the report of intelligence to Lord Minto in advance of the invasion of Java. As Noltie continues, 'This less than generous behaviour of Raffles thus existed long before his public falling out with Farquhar, (whom Raffles referred to as the Old Testament prophet King Malachi), over the administration of Singapore in 1822; the silence became deafening when a widow*- came to promote the posthumous reputation of a beloved husband'.

A further incident where Raffles seemed sanguine about ignoring the contribution made by Farquhar is in relation to the sending of a specimen of a dugong to London. Raffles had dissected a dugong and sent details to London whereas Farquhar had obtained an actual specimen and sent it to Calcutta. Unbeknownst to Farquhar, Raffles, who just happened to be in Calcutta at the time, sent the unhappily deceased dugong to the London Zoological Society omitting any reference to Farquhar, where the specimen is recorded as having been sent by Mr Raffles.

Family Life
We know little of Farquhar's family life. When he was in Malacca, in common with many emigrants, he took a local wife. He lived with Antoinette Clement or Clemaine, known as Nonya or Nonio, believed to be of Malaccan-French descent and the daughter of a French customs officer. The date of the marriage is not known, indeed whether it was a formal marriage is likewise unknown. How they met is not recorded anywhere although Farquhar first arrived in Malacca not long after his escapades in the attack on Pondicherry.

William Farquhar arrived in Malacca in 1795, by which time both his parents had died, his father Robert in 1773 at the age of 50 and his mother Agnes in 1782 at the young age of 46. Farquhar was present at the formal surrender and transfer of Malacca from the Dutch. He was recalled temporarily to Madras in 1797 to take part in an expedition to Manila, which did not ultimately take place, and he returned to Malacca in 1797. He had wasted no time in taking a local woman as a wife but this was no temporary fling as no doubt many military men had made in postings all over the British Empire. Farquhar and Antoinette remained together until he departed from

*Much of the detail of Raffles' life is brought to us by the work of his second wife Sophia who penned the *Memoir of the Life and Public Services of Sir Thomas Stamford Raffles* in 1830. Sophia's biography is flawed in that it omits entirely key facts of his life, including Raffles's first wife Olivia, to whom he was married for nine years.

A young girl of the East Indies, 1800s.

Singapore on 27 December 1823, close to 28 years together.

John Thomson the Scottish photographer from Edinburgh who travelled widely in the East and set up a Singapore studio in 1862, eloquently paints a lyrical picture of the charms of the women of Malacca in his book, *The Strait of Malacca, Indo-China and China: Or, Ten Years' Travels, Adventures, and Residence Abroad,* which was published 1875.

'Should any warm-hearted bachelor wish, he might furnish himself with a pretty and attractive-looking wife from among the daughters of that sunny clime; but let him make no long stay there if indisposed to marry, unless he can defy the witchery of soft dark eyes, of raven tresses, and of sylph-like forms. It is a spot where leisure seems to sit at every man's doorway; drowsy as the placid sea, and idle as the huge palms, whose broad leaves nod above the old weather beaten smug-looking houses'.

Farquhar, as a long-term resident, was clearly beguiled and smitten by the dark eyes and raven tresses.

William Farquhar and Antoinette had six children together, the first of whom is recorded as Esther, born in September 1796. Antoinette was born in 1780 making her 16 years old and Farquhar 22 at the time of the firstborn. Esther was married to Francis James Bernard whom Farquhar had appointed temporarily as Master Attendant until Raffles's own brother-in-law Flint took over that position.

Raffles was probably a prude and a snob. However reprehensible it might seem in retrospect, not only was it common practice to cohabit with local women it was actively encouraged by the employers such as the East India Company and other major trading companies in other parts of the world. Professor T Devine in his book, *To the Ends of the Earth: Scotland's Global Diaspora*, 1750-2010, writing specifically on the Hudson Bay Company which did so much to explore Canada and exploit its wealth of fur and minerals, points out that, the Governor of the HBC, Sir George Simpson, 'expressly advised "connubial alliances" with Indian women, arguing that they are the best security we can have of the good will of the natives.' He added, 'By the 1830's almost all officers in the HBC and many lower-level employees had some kind of relationship with Indian women'. The Indian referred to here is, of course, the native American. The situation in the East was unlikely to be any different.

Whatever the basis of the relationship and regardless of how long it existed, cultural differences and prejudices would arise when the time came to return home. Sometimes, traders would create a new home and remain but soldiers and administrators were servants of the Crown or employees of a company by which they were engaged and subject to retirement, postings and transfers to other territories.

Some 'wives' would simply be abandoned and forgotten, creating anguished scenarios such as are now played out by Cio Cio and Pinkerton on stages across the world. Some would however, be remembered and provided for in some way. In Farquhar's case he did make provision in his will for property to be left to his 'wife'.

The fate of their first-born Esther is the distressing result of the attitudes of the time. In spite of being married to the son-in-law of the co-founder of the settlement and Francis himself being the first commander of a police force in Singapore and the founder of *The Singapore Chronicle*, things did not turn out well for Esther. Francis left Singapore on a trading ship in 1827 and never returned. His death in Batavia or Jakarta was recorded in the newspaper in December 1843. The unfortunate Esther was left destitute and petitioned the East India Company for support. She died in July 1838 at the age of 41 just months before her own father who had made some specific provisions for her in his will. It is a reflection of the difficulty in communication that Farquhar seemed to be unaware of the depths of Esther's circumstances.

It is known, however, that Esther's children visited their grandfather in Perth, Scotland and were partly educated there. They survived and emigrated eventually to Canada. It has been revealed recently that Margaret Trudeau, wife of the celebrated Prime Minister of Canada, Pierre Trudeau, is the great great great great granddaughter of William Farquhar through the line of Esther and Francis.

Andrew, the eldest son of William Farquhar, who had moved from Malacca to Singapore in 1820, invested in property and owned a two-acre site at the corner of Middle Road and North Bridge Road in Singapore, close to his father's residence on Beach Road. He married Elizabeth Robinson and with three children moved to the new property. In 1827, Andrew was appointed as coroner but in January 1829, on a visit to Jakarta, which for some inexplicable reason he had undertaken to improve his health, he died. Elizabeth was better provided for than poor Esther, benefitting from the property acquired by her husband.

A Retired Life

In spite of the long relationship with Antoinette, it was Farquhar alone who left Singapore at the end of December 1823 to return to Scotland. He settled in Perth just over 40 miles north of Edinburgh where he had two houses built at Early Bank in 1828, one for him and one for his brother Arthur. Perth was not his hometown which was in Aberdeenshire, but in the absence of his parents and, at the time of his return, no other local dependants, he was free to chose where he would settle. Perth is centrally placed in Scotland, just north of the more heavily populated central belt and south of the 'highland line' which consists mainly of mountainous land and small rural communities. In the 1830s, it would be a fine country town at the banks of the River Tay.

Sir Walter Scott describes it in his novel, *The Fair Maid of Perth*, written when Farquhar was living in that city in 1831. The opening lines of Scott's novel are, 'Among all the provinces in Scotland, if an intelligent stranger were asked to describe the most varied and the most beautiful, it is probable he would name the county of Perth.' He added that 'Perthshire forms the fairest portion of the northern kingdom', it 'exhibits the varied beauties of natural scenery in greatest perfection,' home to not the highest but the most picturesque hills and rivers which find their way out of the mountains by the 'wildest leaps' and through the 'most romantic passes'.

Farquhar, after the heat and dust of India, the humidity of Singapore and the pressures of duty, would surely have appreciated the wide vistas of a country town which had not been blighted by the industrial revolution as many southern towns had, and would have admired 'the valley of the Tay, traversed by its two large meadows, or Inches, its steeples, and its towers; the hills of Moncrieff and Kinnoul faintly rising into the picturesque rocks, partly clothed with woods; the rich margin of the river, studded with elegant mansions; and the distant view of the huge Grampian mountains, the northern screen of this exquisite landscape.' Indeed, the 'elegant mansions' he described would eventually include those of Major Farquhar at Early Bank.

Back in his homeland, Farquhar wasted little time in seeking out a wife and, at the age of 54 years on 7 April of 1828, he married Margaret Lobban from Fochabers, Scotland. This union produced six children, one son and five daughters. Margaret Lobban was born on 10 July 1808 and baptised one day after, conscious perhaps that lives at that time could be brought to a sudden halt through disease or infection. Her mother was Isabel Laing and her father Robert Lobban, a shipwright who was just two years older than Farquhar. William and Margaret were married in St Mary's Church, Marleybone, London. At the tender age of 19, she was 'given away by her brother-in-law John Booth, a house painter from Aberdeen, husband of Margaret's

Margaret Lobban. (Copyright Anna Loake 2010. Reproduced by kind permission of Anna Loake.)

sister Ellen. The best man was the groom's brother, Arthur Farquhar R.N., a distinguished naval officer who would be knighted four years later, and retire as Rear-Admiral.'

There is no information available on how they met and why they were married. It was not unusual for the times for men to be older than their bride but the gap in this instance of over 30 years is out of the ordinary. Nor do we know why London was chosen as the venue for an important occasion for Scottish families. Margaret had seven sisters and it is doubtful if they were all able to travel for the occasion.

A portrait of Margaret shows her as a fine-looking young woman with delicate features and a tousled bouffant of dark hair piled above a pale oval face with dark eyes and just a hint of a smile. A long graceful neck, unadorned by jewellery, ends at the wide-collars of a dark empire line dress with wide pink edging. She is holding on her lap a young blonde haired girl in a white dress who is holding up her hand. Perhaps this is one of the daughters of William and Margaret.

Farquhar's son William Grant, born in March 1829, the year that Farquhar retired officially from the East India Company, followed his father's footsteps and joined the Indian Army. One daughter died a few days after birth and three other daughters died before the age of 30. Amelia, born in 1834, the longest lived, married a banker from Aberdeen, Robert Lumsden and had two children, Oswald and Amelia. The older Amelia died on 22 August 1914, just three weeks after the start of hostilities in the First World War.

Lieutenant W G Farquhar, Major Farquhar's son, whilst in the Madras Artillery and Engineers, kept contact with his sisters by writing letters and maintaining a diary which he would send home every so often. The letters are warm, indicating close family ties.

His diary entries and letters refer frequently to the stifling heat, injuries sustained and death from disease of his fellow soldiers whilst engaged in actions in Burma and various parts of India.

His letters have a lighthearted touch as well. In one to Amelia dated 14 May 1856, he referred to a new doctor and his wife arriving. They are both 'Scotch' and he commented on the 'Edinburgh twang' of the wife which he had not heard for a long time. He regreted the absence of Scottish girls, 'I don't know why but I have met very few Scotch girls in India'. He continued, 'Isn't it odd that there are not more Scotch ladies? Of Scotch men there is a very unfair proportion so say the English. It is true of the Doctors I am sure for almost every one you meet hails from the land of cakes.*'

Lt Farquhar died of cholera in India at the age of 31 in 1860. He had been keen to gain promotion to Adjutant and passed the requisite Hindustani language exams, but promotion was not forthcoming. It was a two-edged sword as promotion would have meant giving up a well-deserved and much-needed furlough.

Major-General William Farquhar made a Will and Testament to dispose of his property on his death. It is a considerably lengthy document, running to almost 50 pages, including a codicil and an inventory of property on his death. The main will is written in 1833 and clearly anticipates considerable value of his property and business interests. He refers to properties purchased from the Moncrieff Estates, (local major landowners and a distinguished old Scottish family in Perthshire), and two merchants in Perth. It is possible that these purchases simply comprised the new estate he was creating for himself at Early Bank, much of which has since been split up and overbuilt.

The main features of the will are to provide the Scottish property and estates for his wife Margaret with a series of provisions about remarrying, the creation of a trust fund from which various allowances and annuities would be paid and an instruction to his trustees to, 'upon my decease convey and make over to Nonio Clement presently or lately residing at Sincapore and mother of my natural children in the East Indies if in life at the time of my death in absolute property that house belonging to me in Camponglam in Sincapore presently or lately possessed by her together with the whole furniture and other effects therein to be disposed of by her at pleasure'.

Farquhar's house in Kampong Glam was in a prestigious location, near as it would be to the Sultan's palace and grounds, within easy reach of the main business areas of the settlement on the river. His residence gave its name to the road in which it was placed – Farquhar Street – but subsequent development in the area in 1994 has erased the only road in Singapore named after him from the map.

From the trust fund, which was to be created on his death from sale of assets, he made provision for an annuity to his Singapore wife of 350 Spanish

---

*Scotland is known as the Land of Cakes based on its traditional reliance on the humble oatcake for sustenance and survival. The name was first mentioned poetically by Robert Fergusson (1750-1774) in his poem 'The King's Birthday in Edinburgh'. 'Oh, soldiers! For your ain dear sakes For Scotland's, alias, Land o' Cakes'

Dollars payable half yearly in advance, and to his daughter Esther Bernard the interest on 1,000 pounds annually. Furthermore, the trustees were directed to ensure this latter sum should be allocated for her aliment alone and specifically not for her present or any future husband or any debts which they might incur. It seems unusual that he seems unaware of the situation of Esther who was clearly in need of money at the time the will is drawn up and indeed the codicil predates her death by only a few months.

The codicil to the will comes in January 1838 and refers to the 'great change in my circumstances occasioned by the failure of my Agents in Calcutta and London'. He changes the trustees and removes all of the various legacies and annuities. The support for his wife is reduced and the support for Antoinette Clement and Esther is left to the discretion of the trustees should resources permit. The legacy of the house and property in Kampong Glam, is reduced to a liferent.*

Farquhar had a quiet life in Perth. There are few records of any of his activities and he must have enjoyed the relaxed life in a rural community with his young wife and new family after the constant trial of army life from a young age and then the pressure of administration, management and development of settlements in Malacca and Singapore. In addition to purchasing the two houses at Early Bank, he had a billiard room built in the grounds and one can imagine that he would enjoy a quiet game with his brother Arthur, away from the noise of his young children and those of Esther when they came to stay.

His health, however, did start to give some concern and a letter from him dated 21 November 1835 to a James Morison, the purveyor and creator of 'Morison's Vegetable Universal Medicine', indicates his faith in the eponymous pills. Morison was born in Aberdeenshire, Scotland in 1770; not trained as a doctor, he called himself a Hygeist and established a business based on his theory that, 'Blood forms the body – Air gives it Life.' The efficacy of his vegetable pills was questionable, consisting mainly of purgative substances, and although they sold extraordinarily well, Mr Morison was much lampooned in the press and society in general. His pills were referred to in Dickens' novels and a Morison pill became a byword and synonym for a cure-all in any circumstance. They were widely distributed and used throughout the world; the list of agents for the medicament was six pages

---

*A liferent allows occupation of property until death after which the property reverts to the estate.

long. Thomas Carlyle the Scottish philosopher and writer, famously comments in *Past and Present*, 'Brothers, I am sorry I have got no Morrison's Pill [sic] for curing the maladies of society'.

In his letter, Farquhar informed us that he suffered a 'paralytic affection of the left side, for the relief of which I underwent all the usual remedies prescribed in such complaints by the faculty. The complaint was accompanied by a termination of blood to the head, and frequent bleedings and cupping, and latterly a seton* was introduced to the back of my neck; in the course of time I recovered so far as to be able to proceed to London, where I consulted Sir Henry Halford, but I found that he could afford me no farther relief'.

He also refers to a loss of voice due to tremulous motion in his lower jaw, the use of leeches on a regular basis to control various symptoms and 'disagreeable eruptions' which broke out all over his legs and his face. His letter ends on a rather forlorn note as he concluded sadly, 'I lead a very retired life, seldom dining abroad, – my age is 62.' However, Morison's Pills seem to have done the trick and on 25 January 1836, he wrote once again to Morison praising the efficacy of the pills, of which he is now taking 20 a day, and said that the eruptions on his legs have now gone and the soreness in his eyes much improved.

Clearly a broken man after a lifetime of work in the service of the East India Company, effectively the Crown, without the recognition he deserved for his contribution to the founding and development of the new settlement at Singapore, his stalwart work before and during the invasion of Java and his effective stewardship of Malacca, he found himself ignored and in severely reduced circumstances. Just over a year after the codicil is registered, he died on 11 May 1839, leaving his 30-year-old widow and young family. The clerk in the Registry, recording the death, managed to get the date of death wrong and badly misspelled Farquhar's name and rank; consequently the date in the Perth newspaper, *The Courier*, is also incorrect. The local historian in Perth commented, 'the clerk who recorded that had very eccentric spelling even by the standard of the time'.

The cause of death is recorded as 'apoplexy' which today would be classed as a stroke bearing in mind the symptoms which Farquhar had suffered from.

On the date of his death, his inventory of effects in Scotland, excluding property, is valued at less than 1,000 pounds; about 20,000 pounds sterling at today's rates. Shortly after his death, his widow Margaret sold the property in

---

*A medical procedure used to aid healing of fistulae.

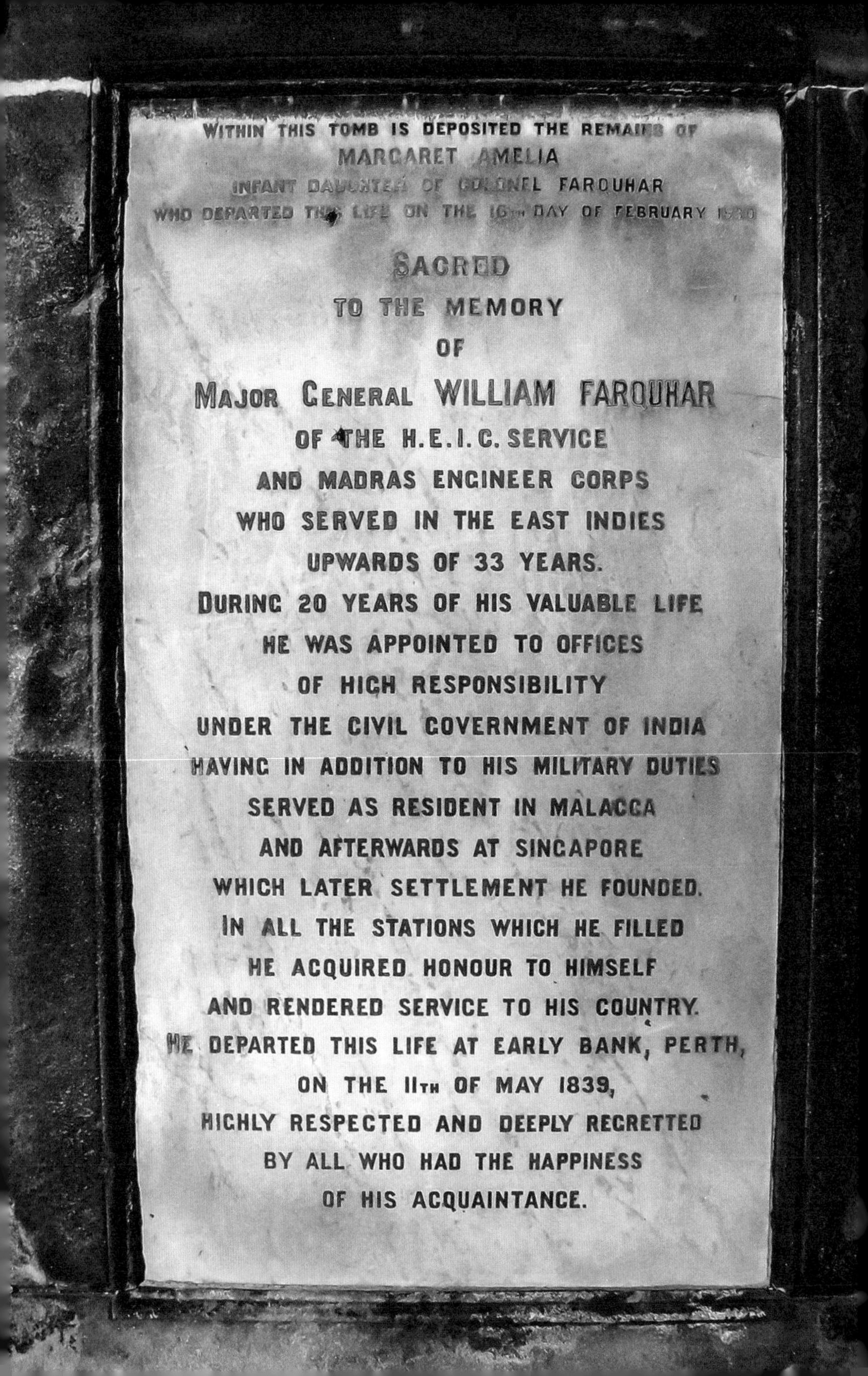

WITHIN THIS TOMB IS DEPOSITED THE REMAINS OF
MARGARET AMELIA
INFANT DAUGHTER OF COLONEL FARQUHAR
WHO DEPARTED THIS LIFE ON THE 16TH DAY OF FEBRUARY 1830

SACRED
TO THE MEMORY
OF
MAJOR GENERAL WILLIAM FARQUHAR
OF THE H.E.I.C. SERVICE
AND MADRAS ENGINEER CORPS
WHO SERVED IN THE EAST INDIES
UPWARDS OF 33 YEARS.
DURING 20 YEARS OF HIS VALUABLE LIFE
HE WAS APPOINTED TO OFFICES
OF HIGH RESPONSIBILITY
UNDER THE CIVIL GOVERNMENT OF INDIA
HAVING IN ADDITION TO HIS MILITARY DUTIES
SERVED AS RESIDENT IN MALACCA
AND AFTERWARDS AT SINGAPORE
WHICH LATER SETTLEMENT HE FOUNDED.
IN ALL THE STATIONS WHICH HE FILLED
HE ACQUIRED HONOUR TO HIMSELF
AND RENDERED SERVICE TO HIS COUNTRY.
HE DEPARTED THIS LIFE AT EARLY BANK, PERTH,
ON THE 11TH OF MAY 1839,
HIGHLY RESPECTED AND DEEPLY REGRETTED
BY ALL WHO HAD THE HAPPINESS
OF HIS ACQUAINTANCE.

Perth and returned to her homeland of Fochabers where she died in January 1844. His Singapore wife Antoinette Nonio Clement outlived both, dying in Singapore in 1852.

Legacy

William Farquhar was entombed in a modest mausoleum in a quiet corner near the entrance to the historic Grey Friars Churchyard in the Fair City of Perth. It holds the inscription: 'In addition to his military duties, served as Resident in Malacca and afterwards at Singapore which later settlement he founded.'

Farquhar's legacy to Singapore is difficult to quantify. How can one measure the effort, skill, professionalism and sheer grit it must have taken to establish a colony in the face of outright hostility from the Dutch, initial indifference by the East India Company, alarm from the British Government, and an absentee, self-proclaimed 'founder' who fired off missives with no understanding of the situation on the ground. The old soldier's adage, that no battle plan survives the first encounter with the enemy, is apt in the context of developing a new settlement. It is not possible to plan it on paper alone.

Not a single memorial remains in Singapore to Farquhar's name save the botanical and zoological paintings and the silver epergne presented by the residents of Singapore, both now housed in the National Museum.

Farquhar was present from the outset of the development of colonial Singapore. He was involved in the deliberations which resulted in Singapore being selected as the most appropriate location for the new East India Company settlement, and at the negotiation of treaties and, most importantly, had put into practice with minimal supervision the ideas which resulted in the successful port for the East India Company. The stage was set for the next Resident to develop that legacy.

DR JOHN CRAWFURD

When Farquhar was deposed unceremoniously by Raffles in 1823, he was immediately succeeded by Dr John Crawfurd (sometimes spelt as Crawford). Crawfurd, a fellow Scot, was a physician born in 1783 on Islay, an island off the west coast of Scotland famed for its variety of superior whisky distilleries. It has a land area very similar to that of Singapore but boasts only a few thousand inhabitants.

William Farquhar's tombstone. (Photo: David Bonnar)

Following a family tradition, he studied medicine and completed his studies at the renowned Edinburgh University medical school in 1803 at the age of 20. Shortly after that, he was engaged by the East India Company as a company surgeon and posted to India until 1808 when he moved to Penang where he first encountered Stamford Raffles.

He accompanied Raffles, Minto and others on the invasion of Java in 1811 where he was appointed Resident at Yogyakarta in November 1811. He was a scholarly man and studied Javanese and the local culture. He was invaluable to Raffles in his administration of Java although he disagreed strongly with Raffles's plans to reform the land system.

When Java was returned to the Dutch in 1816, Crawfurd returned home to Britain and, in 1820, he published much of his studies in a three volume history of the Indian Archipelago. His work brought him to the attention of Hastings, the Governor-General of India and in between postings to Siam and Vietnam, he took up the residency at Singapore. Crawfurd's work was diplomatically vital to Britain's interests in Southeast Asia as well as proving to be a valued resource for scholars.

Crawfurd arrived in Singapore on 27 May 1823 and was received by a guard-of-honour and a 15-gun salute; he took command of the Resident's office on 9 June that year. Raffles left Singapore that same day for Bencoolen and never again set foot in Singapore having been in the new settlement only three times.

In spite of Crawfurd's undoubted abilities, he had a hard act to follow. Farquhar was popular and had no doubt introduced ways of working which people had become used to and at any rate, few like a new broom. Buckley is blunt in his assessment and said Crawfurd was unpopular and a 'typical scotchman', whose frugality was apt to degenerate into parsimoniousness. In other words he was mean. However, Buckley added, with faint praise, that he 'managed the affairs of the settlement with energy and ability'.

Walter Scott Duncan, a Shetlander who travelled to Singapore in 1823, kept a diary of his sojourn and he was also less than complimentary about the attributes of his fellow Scot. Attending a dinner to honour the founding of the settlement, Duncan recounted, 'A little after ten we rose from the table, but not before we had apparently exhausted the Resident's stores, for during the last hour there had been a constant outcry for wine, which was little attended to.' When a toast was called for, the Resident himself had to borrow a bottle of claret and Duncan refers to his 'ill timed frugality'. However, Duncan seemed over zealous in his criticism as he also berated the rest

Dr John Crawfurd. (National Portrait Gallery, London)

of the party for their lack of ability in public speaking, low intellect and lack of good humour.

Crawfurd was in charge of the settlement from 9 June 1823 until 14 August 1826 during which time the port continued to prosper and grow. A population census taken at this time indicated a total of 10,683: 74 were European, 3,317 Chinese, 6,505 Malay and Bugis, 756 Indian and the rest Arab and Armenian. Issues to be resolved include ensuring fresh water was available to ships, flooding due to high tides and continuing land allocation and tenure.

Duncan, in his diary, also referred to Crawfurd's inability to follow through on an order he had posted – that Malays should not be permitted to openly carry the kris following the murder of two Chinese men. Duncan observed that the instruction was largely ignored. The Resident sent a peon to the Sultan to inform him of the ruling and, in a true expression of shooting the messenger, the Sultan threatened to kill the peon if he ever appeared with such a message again. A subsequent visit to the Sultan by the Resident himself made no more headway and the matter seemed to have been dropped. Duncan probably did not understand the cultural significance of the situation and the potent symbolism of the kris, and again seemed unreasonably harsh in his criticism of Crawfurd. Already the mythical qualities and legacy of Raffles seem to have swayed Duncan in his views and he extols Raffles's virtues in comparison with Crawfurd's achievements which he unfairly belittles.

One of the continuing questions which caused argument between Raffles and Crawfurd in the same way as it had with Farquhar, was the question of gambling and whether it should be permitted. There were two schools of thought then, indeed as there are now. These were, to allow gambling but to license it and derive some government excise from it, or to ban it on the grounds that it is morally unacceptable. Again, then as now, the argument for banning it entirely was challenged on the grounds that it was a harmless amusement and, if not permitted legally, it would occur illegally and what is more, promote crime and cause corruption in the police and other authorities. After much discussion, the gambling was abolished by the Court of Directors of the East India Company in 1829 and, as predicted by Dr Crawfurd, caused loss of income and corruption.

Crawfurd was critical of the early treaties made by Raffles. He pointed out somewhat condescendingly, 'It does not appear to me that the influence of the native chiefs has in any respect been necessary or even beneficial in the formation, maintenance, or progress of this settlement, the prosperity of which has rested solely and exclusively on the character and resources of the British Government'. He goes on to say that the only sensible solution would be to negotiate for sovereignty over the entire island to avoid any implications in the future that local chiefs could resile from any land transactions or indeed any aspect of the existing agreement. The Raffles treaties, in Crawfurd's opinion, had been deficient in a number of ways and he asked for the right to renegotiate for complete cession of the island. The Governor-General of India replied on 5 March 1824 in complete concurrence.

By 2 August 1824, Crawfurd had, on behalf of the East India Company, and by implication, the British government, negotiated for a complete transfer of the island. Article Two of the Treaty records that their Highnesses cede in full sovereignty and property to the Honourable East India Company, for ever, the Island of Singapore together with the adjacent seas, straits and islets. All previous treaties were annulled.

This significant achievement solved at a stroke many of the major issues facing the still new settlement. Land tenure could be assured, defence issues were clear for the long term and long-term development of the colony could proceed without any anxiety.

Slavery, the cause of much animosity between Farquhar and Raffles, had until the new Treaty, remained unresolved; slavery was illegal in Britain but not under Malay law and practice. Crawfurd's view was that if it was not acceptable in Britain nor should it be acceptable in any of her possessions. Crawfurd recognised that servitude arising from a combination of debt and traditions of allegiance to chiefs might have to be treated sensitively. However, he stated, 'I have not permitted the present Treaty to be polluted even by the mention of the subject'. He continued, 'under these favourable circumstances, slavery may be said to be banished from the island.' Crawfurd succeeded by striking at the root of the problem rather than remonstrating with officials who had no real jurisdiction over such matters under the previous arrangements.

The Treaty between Britain and Holland, also concluded in 1824, resolved many of the wider issues regarding territory and trade in Southeast Asia, including removal of the Dutch objection to the settlement at Singapore. This combined with Crawfurd's Treaty effectively opened the way for unfettered expansion and development of Singapore.

A year after the treaty was signed, Crawfurd formally took possession of the island by circumnavigating it in the ship *Malabar* in four days.

Overleaf: Singapore town from Government Hill, 1828.

Around that time, he ascended Bukit Timah Hill, previously unclimbed by any known individual, and fired 21 gun salutes on Pulau Ubin and Coney Islands. Crawfurd, the cantankerous verging on parsimonious Scot, had through his considerable skill and diplomacy, not only continued to steer the island to further prosperity at a time when a prompt reply to a letter from Britain took nine months, but dealt with the major problems of land tenure, gambling and slavery and ultimately rendered his greatest service to Britain, which was to negotiate and conclude the treaty which ceded the entire territory and sovereignty and allowed the continued and future development of Singapore.

After leaving his post in Singapore, Dr Crawfurd was appointed to a mission in Burma. Upon his retirement, he made an unsuccessful attempt to enter the British Parliament through a Glasgow seat and continued writing on his experiences and travels. He died in London at the age of 85 in 1868. His contribution to the development of Singapore is recognized here in the naming of Crawford Street, Crawford Bridge and Crawford Park.

If it was Raffles who outlined the principles of Singapore, albeit borrowed from others, and Farquhar who created it and built the solid foundations from which later expansion became possible, it was Crawfurd who set the seal on the permanence of the venture by securing the entire island.

The scene is then set for the development of Singapore. An important part had already been played by Scotsmen and to fully understand the reasons for their coming to Singapore and the East in significant numbers, we should review a little of the history of that country.

The start of Crawford Street at Crawford Bridge which spans the Kallang River.

TWO

A Brief History of Scotland

Nine thousand to 12,000 years ago, Scotland was covered by the last of the great ice sheets and only as it drew back were successive waves of people drawn to the north. Tribes from northern Europe, and Scandinavians from across the seas comprised its first peoples. A nation of immigrants from the start, further influx from Flanders, Poland and the Baltic states added to the colourful mosaic of cultures which is today's Scotland.

The Roman occupation of Britain, starting in 43 AD and lasting until 410 AD, failed to make much of an impact on Caledonia, as Scotland was known by the Romans. Apart from forays into the Scottish lowlands, the northern limit of the permanently occupied Roman Empire ended at Hadrian's Wall, whose construction started in 122 AD. It was the most heavily fortified border in the Roman Empire which is closely coincident with the current Scottish border with England.

Dio Cassius, a Roman commentator, said of the Scots in 197 AD: 'They live in huts, go naked and unshod. They mostly have a democratic government, and are much addicted to robbery. They can bear hunger and cold and all manner of hardship; they will retire into their marshes and hold out for days with only their heads above water, and in the forest they will subsist on barks and roots.'

Survival must have been a tough business in a northern land with poor weather and little arable land. As a result, warlike tribes with allegiances to local chieftains created a martial culture.

Wars of Independence
During the 13th and 14th centuries, Scotland was subject to invasion from England and a war of independence was fought aggressively by both parties. Legends developed from historical figures such as William Wallace who, having won a major battle at Stirling Bridge in 1297, was later defeated at Falkirk and subsequently captured in 1305, taken to England and brutally

The Matthew Paris map of Scotland, 1250.

hanged, drawn and quartered.

Wallace's heroism and execution has earned him iconic status and he became the subject of ballads, stories and song which embellished his already considerable achievement.

Robert the Bruce, born in 1274, became King of Scots in 1306 and reigned until his death in 1329. Accepted as one of the greatest of Scottish heroes, he led Scotland to independence by his major victory over Edward the First of England, at the Battle of Bannockburn in 1314. It is no accident that the present Scottish government wished to hold a referendum vote on independence in the year 2014, the 700th anniversary of this famed battle.

The year 1320 saw the Declaration of Arbroath, the first ever written declaration of independence, which states its relationship with England loudly and clearly as the following extract illustrates: 'for, as long as but a hundred of us remain alive, never will we on any conditions be brought under English rule. It is in truth not for glory, nor riches, nor honours that we are fighting, but for freedom – for that alone, which no honest man gives up but with life itself.'

Scotland was active in making friends in Europe. In 1295, much to the chagrin of England who quarreled with all of their neighbours, an alliance with the French was made which lasted until 1560 when the Treaty of Edinburgh, in the wake of the Scottish Reformation, brought together England and Scotland in common cause for the first time.

A Hardy People

Much of the early economy of Scotland was based on cattle rearing. It was not of the breeds we are familiar with today but the black highland cattle, small and sturdy, requiring time to mature and grow. Cattle raiding from neighbouring clans became prevalent and raiding into England from the Scottish borders led to many skirmishes and small-scale wars. Two verses from the anonymous ballad celebrating the Battle of Otterbourne in 1388 illustrate this:

> *It fell about the Lammas tide, When the muir-men win their hay,*
> *The doughty earl of Douglas rode Into England, to catch a prey.*
> *And he has burn'd the dales of Tyne, And part of Bambrough shire;*
> *And three good towers on Roxburgh fells, He left them all on fire.*

To bring cattle to market, they were driven from the north of Scotland and the outlying islands, across the sound of Sleat from the island of Skye to fatten and sell in markets of the south. Cattle drovers became familiar figures and drovers' inns such as Inveroran, Inverarnan and Kingshouse remain to-day as testament to the trails taken by these hardy men. Huge trysts or fairs, such as the one at Falkirk in central Scotland, became centres of trading and exchange before further droves were made down to the bigger markets such as Smithfield in London.

Sir Walter Scott, in his novel *The Two Drovers* gives a flavour of the droving trade and those who practised it.

'It was the day after Doune Fair when my story commences. It had been a brisk market, several dealers had attended from the northern and mid-land counties in England, and English money had flown so merrily about as to gladden the hearts of the Highland farmers. Many large droves were about to set off for England, under the protection of their owners, or of the topsmen whom they employed in the tedious, laborious, and responsible office of driving the cattle for many hundred miles, from the market where they had been purchased, to the fields or farm-yards where they were to be fattened for the shambles.

Above: Drovers at rest. Overleaf: (left) The Declaration of Arbroath dated 1320, (right) Robert the Bruce.

'The Highlanders in particular are masters of this difficult trade of driving, which seems to suit them as well as the trade of war. It affords exercise for all their habits of patient endurance and active exertion. They are required to know perfectly the drove-roads, which lie over the wildest tracts of the country, and to avoid as much as possible the highways, which distress the feet of the bullocks, and the turnpikes, which annoy the spirit of the drover; whereas on the broad green or grey track, which leads across the pathless moor, the herd not only move at ease and without taxation, but, if they mind their business, may pick up a mouthful of food by the way. At night, the drovers usually sleep along with their cattle, let the weather be what it will; and many of these hardy men do not once rest under a roof during a journey on foot from Lochaber to Lincolnshire.'

The Union of the Crowns

In 1603, Queen Elizabeth I of England died unwed and without having produced an heir. However, previous intermarriage between the royal families of England and Scotland had created an acceptable line of succession to the English throne. James, King of Scotland, was a first cousin, twice removed, of the late Queen Elizabeth.

James VI of Scotland thus succeeded Elizabeth and became James I of England. James moved his court to England and initiated a process of gradual integration which he hoped would lead to political union and the creation of a single country. This was not a popular move and in spite of various commissions established to investigate the possibilities, the two kingdoms remained separate until 1707 when, for a variety of reasons, a Treaty of Union was enacted in both countries and the United Kingdom of Great Britain was created.

The Act of Union 1707

The motivation of the two countries at this time was complicated. However, it can be argued that the principal drivers were, on the English side, the desire to avoid a situation where Scotland, should succession issues arise again, might choose its own king and thereby create the potential for future alliances against English interests and, particularly, to avoid a Catholic succession. On the Scottish side, one major contributor to the change of perspective was a then ill-fated colonial adventure to the Isthmus of Panama in central America, known as the Darien Scheme, which caused massive and unprecedented losses to its many investors and a serious loss of confidence in the nation as a whole.

Sir Walter Scott in a portrait by Sir William Allan, 1844.

Parliaments at this time were not the bastions of people's representation which they purport to be nowadays, but consisted largely of vested interests in land, aristocracy and business. General opposition amongst ordinary people to the union was high and the disdain held for those in power, who had in popular opinion sold Scottish birthright, was captured aptly in Burns famous lines from 'Sic a Parcel o' Rogues in a Nation' which are quoted often to this day:

> Fareweel to a' our Scot'tish fame,
> Fareweel our ancient glory;
> Fareweel to e'en our Scottish name
> Sae famed in sang and story.
> But, pith and power, till my last hour,
> I'll make this declaration:
> We were bought and sold for English gold!
> Sic a parcel o' rogues in a nation!

Sir Walter Scott, the novelist, is less poetic but more succinct when, in his introduction to *Rob Roy*, he refers to the Union as 'that most obnoxious of measures'. Burns probably represented accurately the contempt that was held for the legislators and those entrusted with the stewardship of Scotland. However, in retrospect, Burns is too quick to write off the nation and the will of its people to sustain and add to the fame, glory and name of Scotland. The intention might have been to lose the name of Scotland in some parliamentary sleight of hand; the ambiguous and derogatorily innocuous North Britain was mooted as a possibility; and although many did turn their backs on history, including some of the 19th century Scottish adventurers we come across in the development of Singapore who fashionably refer to themselves as English, there is no getting away from the fact of their birth, ancestry and education which history has not forgotten.

The Act of Union in 1707 is often misunderstood. It did not create a single country, merely a single Parliament leaving Scotland and England as two sovereign states. However, after the Act, many Scots did behave as if they had become part of England and even referred to the entire country as England in the way that many foreigners do today, unaware of the historical situation and the sensitivities of national feeling. The term "British" took longer to come into regular use. Scotland retained its core identity through its own legal, church and education systems, its languages of Scots and Gaelic however, started a long and slow decline.

Top right: Scotland from the Ortelius map, c 1603. Bottom right: The Downsitting of the Scottish Parliament, c 1680s.

Education

Schools in Scotland began to be founded in the 12th and 13th century and universities in the 15th and 16th centuries. In 1801, with an estimated population of 1.6 million, Scotland had already four universities and many respected schools.

Scottish scholars were known to travel to both teach and study at continental universities such as Paris and Leiden, and opened a route to new lines of thought which were brought back to Scotland. England was for many years bypassed because access to England's two universities was precluded following the 14th century wars of independence.

The first Education Act in 1496 was concerned with ensuring that the gentry had perfect Latin but subsequent legislation in 1616, 1633 and 1646 widened the intention to include a school in every parish. In the 16th century, Andrew Melville, educated in Poitiers, Paris, and returned from Geneva, reformed both the school and university systems to make them equal in standing to any of those in continental Europe. This work was a sound foundation for the implementation of the *First Book of Discipline* and the work of John Knox in 1560.

New ideas of humanism were brought into public Scottish life and the role of the universities and the frequent contact with Europe led to the development of philosophical ideas which encouraged the flowering of thought and science known as the Scottish Enlightenment.

The Scottish Enlightenment saw a remarkable outpouring of original thinking in a wide range of fields from geology to philosophy, sciences and economics. James Hutton's research into geology and earth formation stimulated others such as Charles Darwin to take a new standpoint on the age of the earth and the effect of time on the creatures inhabiting it. *The Wealth of Nations*, which laid the foundations for an open market economy and the principles of international trade is still regarded today as a seminal work on political economy, was by Adam Smith, a native of Kirkcaldy in Fife. David Hume's philosophy on the nature of knowledge and science and man's place in the world, influenced many thinkers of the day.

A visiting Englishman to Edinburgh standing at Edinburgh Cross was heard to remark at this time that 'I can in a few minutes take 50 men of genius by the hand' and it is of this period that Voltaire said 'we look to Scotland for all our ideas of civilisation'.

This liberation of thinking, viewing man and science from different perspectives than hitherto, opened up discussion and the way to further elaboration of philosophies and science. The already powerful and widespread education system in Scotland meant that the population were well placed to participate and there was a release of energy giving us the work of James Watt, James Clerk Maxwell, Sir James Young Simpson, writers such as Sir Walter Scott, James Hogg and Robert Burns, and scholars such as John Leyden.

Iron and the Industrial Revolution
Iron has been worked for a few thousand years in many places in Scotland, but as a major industry its heyday started in the 18th century. Scotland was well placed to take advantage of its natural resources and availability of iron ores and coal for smelting. These resources were concentrated mainly in the central belt of Scotland: the most densely populated area sandwiched between the highlands to the north and the border country to the south. Proximity to the sea for import and export of raw material and finished goods was an added benefit.

Major production of iron started at the Carron Iron Works near Falkirk in central Scotland in 1759. The invention of the cast-iron blowing cylinder in 1768 and the hot blast process developed at Clyde Iron Works in 1828 gave further impetus to process and production output to meet the demands

Shankers descending a mine shaft, c 1870s.

of the nascent industrial revolution.

Many of the processes used at this time were of course closely guarded secrets and even Robert Burns, Scotland's national poet, in the company of Willie Nicol, the classics master of the Royal High School, Edinburgh, was unable to get in to the Carron foundry at the start of his tour of the highlands in 1787. Rebuffed by the gatekeeper, he retired in a huff to a local hostelry and, using a diamond stylus presented to him by James Cunningham the 14th Earl of Glencairn, etched, somewhat petulantly, the following verse on the window:

> We cam na here to view your warks,
> In hopes to be mair wise,
> But only, lest we go to hell,
> It may be nae surprise:
> But when we tirl'd at your door
> Your porter dought na hear us;
> Sae may, shou'd we to Hell's yetts come,
> Your billy Satan sair us.

The national bard could not affect the ways of these giant foundries which belched out fire and smoke in their ceaseless manufacture of iron for ships, factories and for construction of new machines to produce even more to supply the insatiable demand of the industrial revolution. The towns of the west central belt were all involved in one way or another, coal mining, ore production and processing and digging of canals to transport the materials. Between 1830 and 1847, Scottish iron production leapt from 37,500 tons a year to 540,000 tons, 27 percent of the entire British production.

One town at the centre of this area of Scotland's 'black country' is Coatbridge, Lanarkshire; a description in the book *The Industries of Scotland* by David Bremner gives only a brief glimpse of the horror of pollution, heat, fire and noise: 'Though Coatbridge is a most interesting seat of industry, it is anything but beautiful. Dense clouds of smoke roll over it incessantly; and impart to all the buildings a peculiarly dingy aspect. A coat of black dust overlies everything, and in a few hours the visitor finds his complexion considerably deteriorated by the flakes of soot which fill the air, and settle on his face'.

Coatbridge, in common with many of the surrounding towns and villages in the west of Scotland, has recovered from its historical roots and heavy industry, and no longer defaces its virtues which now boast many recreational facilities and parks.

The social consequences of such 'dark satanic mills' and the Industrial Revolution saw thousands of people displaced from country to town as they sought work in mills, foundries and mines. With housing facilities inadequate to meet the sudden influx and consequent overcrowding creating rapidly developing slum conditions. Displacement on such a scale caused social upheaval and loss of tradition and one of the things which had given Scotland a clear advantage in growth of empire, namely education and literacy, would have begun to suffer. Not surprisingly, public order became a concern as badly treated miners and factory workers with lack of safety and long working hours started to question the status quo.

The treatment of the poor workers in factories across Scotland by overbearing bosses formed a class structure which separated 'gentlemen' and those with the trappings of being a gentleman, that is those with money, from the rest.

The general demand for iron was further fuelled by wars in Europe which needed armaments, in particular cannons. This prompted further growth and adoption of new techniques and processes which, although often invented elsewhere, were first implemented in Scottish foundries.

By 1847, nearly 75 percent of Scottish iron production was exported to England and abroad and Scottish foundry iron was known the world over. Henry Bessemer, the President of the Iron and Steel Institute and inventor of the process for mass production of steel from pig iron, commented during his first visit to Scotland in 1872: 'wherever civilisation had advanced Scottish pig had formed its way.' He was referring, I hope, to the plugs of iron which, when moulded into blocks, had some resemblance to a litter of pigs and hence took the name pig iron.

The deposits of coal and iron were providential and the discovery of a particularly high quality of ironstone in North Lanarkshire, Ayrshire and Stirlingshire, helped to propel the already meteoric rise of the Scottish iron industry. Scotland also led the way in open hearth steel production which produced lighter steel for shipbuilding and that, coupled with the proximity to the sea, led to developments in shipbuilding for which Glasgow and the Clyde became justly famous. In 1861, the town of Clydebank did not exist but by 1901 its population was 30,000. A high proportion of its people would have been engaged in shipbuilding, and as iron replaced wood and steel replaced iron in ship construction, between 1860 and 1870 over 800,000 tons of shipping was built on Clydeside and exported across the globe.

This level of production led to the creation of many companies to take

Overleaf: Shipping on the Clyde by John Grimshaw, 1881.

advantage of the market of the Empire in providing bridges, fountains, and ironware of all description.

Empire and Emigration

Contrary to popular opinion in Scotland, Professor Devine's research, *Scotland's Empire 1600-1815*, confirms that Scots emigrants were not substantially drawn from the poor, disaffected and dispossessed but the educated and landed classes. The evidence points to those from the professions and established families setting forth to make what they could from the empire. This information is borne out in a brief review of the principal Scots who came to Singapore. They included skilled merchants, senior ranking officers of the East India Company and lawyers.

The predominance of Scots arriving in Singapore is a direct reflection of the success of Scots in the higher echelons of the East India Company which dominated business in the East until the loss of its China trade monopoly in 1833. The proportion of Scots in that organisation led to a number of protests and much indignation. Devine reports, 'in the richest of the EIC's provinces, Bengal, between 1774 and 1785, 47 percent of the Writers appointed were Scots, as were 49 percent of the officer cadets and more than 50 percent of the assistant surgeon recruits. All the principal medical officers in Madras were Scots and of the fourteen regiments garrisoning the Indian provinces of the company, seven had been raised in Scotland.'

Although there might have been some outrage and much lampooning in the press at the level of Scots involvement, there was no obvious prejudice against them. Scots, as well as serving in the army and providing the professional and administrative backbone, were investors at the highest levels in the East India Company and direct investors in overseas ventures such as railroads, shipping lines and cattle ranches. They thereby got involved in the overall management as well as the direction of the brains and providing the muscle of the organisation.

John Keay said in his *History of the East India Company*, 'With India itself awash with Campbells, Macleods, MacPhersons and Mackenzies and with both Malacca and the Moluccas under Farquhar rule, it was as if Hastings and Raffles were the only Englishmen around.'

The furthest reaches of Empire were simply new areas for the Scots to travel as they had always done. Prominent positions in London were hard to come by, so ambitious people had to travel further afield to make something of themselves. They had made considerable inroads in America and India, and Southeast Asia was the new frontier, a new adventure.

In theory, there could be no 'British' Empire until after the Union in 1707 of the independent England and Scotland to form the United Kingdom. England had, up to that date, already made strong progress in building colonies, particularly in the Americas, whilst Scotland's attempts at independent colonisation ranged from feeble to catastrophic.

Although it could not be described as British, there is a claim argued by John Keay that the Empire began as early as 1603, the year that the Scottish King, James VI acceded to the English throne. In that year, trader adventurers stepped ashore on the tiny island of Run in the Banda Islands at the Eastern end of the Indonesian archipelago, a home of the nutmeg tree. The success of this enterprise in due course led King James to declare himself King of England, Scotland, Ireland, France, Puloway, (Pulau Ai) and Puloroon, (Pulau Run). The last named, thought one of his visitors, 'could be as valuable to His Majesty as Scotland'.

If a separate Scottish foreign policy became difficult after the Union of the Crowns in 1603, then, after the formal political union, it became impossible. Scotland had always been a country of emigrants and its only route to its own empire was through the ability of its people and their willingness to emigrate and infiltrate, which they did in huge numbers.

Merchants travelled regularly and frequently to the American colonies, low countries, the Baltic states and Poland where significant communities of Scots settled. Continued traditional trade with the Baltic states, the low countries, France and Scandinavia all provided routes for enterprising people to achieve, if not fame and fortune, then at least a reasonable living which a poor country like Scotland was unable to provide to all of its population. Trade included both legitimate business and contraband as many sought to avoid duties on trading of tobacco, for example, from the Americas. The union with England brought Scotland the valuable protection of the Royal Navy and the right to trade without punitive duties and taxes. Within a relatively short period of time after 1707, Glasgow had captured much of the prized tobacco trade acting as an entrepôt for the rest of Europe.

The cultural tradition of military service, the hardy nature of the people fostered by trades such as droving and a poor economy, coupled with high rates of literacy kindled by the Reformation and enriched by the Enlightenment, combined to create the circumstances where Scotland's people provided a disproportionate number of the administrators, officers, teachers, doctors and other professionals of the growing Empire.

THREE

Singapore Landmarks

The proposal to construct a lighthouse on the rocky outcrop of Pedra Branca which commands the entrance to the Singapore Strait, overseeing a significant proportion of the world's shipping, came from a Scot. It was built by a Scot, was dedicated to the memory of a Scot and almost a quarter of the funds to build it was raised by Scots.

> *The Horsburgh Lighthouse is raised by the British enterprise of British Merchants, and by the liberal aid of the East India Company, to lessen the dangers of navigation, and likewise to hand down, so long as it shall last, in the scene of his useful labours. To the Memory of the Great Hydrographer whose name it bears. 1851 WJ Butterworth*

Thus reads the Latin inscription by Butterworth, the Governor of the Straits Settlements 1843-1855, on the Horsburgh Lighthouse on Pedra Branca, confirmed by the Court of International Justice in 2008 as being under the sovereignty of Singapore.

Captain James Horsburgh, 1762-1836
Captain Alexander Hamilton was, in 1703, probably the first Scot to sight and step ashore on Singapore but James Horsburgh must have claim to being one of the most influential early visitors. There is no record of his visits to Singapore itself but it seems unlikely that he did not set foot on the island or at least sail close by at some point.

Sea travel to what was regarded as the outer edges of the world in early days, was reserved for the bold and adventurous and perhaps even foolhardy. Any expansion of trade had to be accompanied by improved navigational methods, charts and lights. Once these were available and in place, the sea routes became safer and faster for merchantmen to ply their trade and for

Background: J T Thomson's 1846 map showing Horsburgh Lighthouse. (Royal Geographic Society) Top inset: J T Thomson's painting of Horsburgh Lighthouse. Bottom inset: Pedra Branca.

the Royal Navy to provide protection.

Horsburgh was born in Elie in the county of Fife, Scotland, a coastal fishing village on the north shores of the wide firth on whose southern shores sits the capital city of Edinburgh. According to Sir Walter Scott in *The Heart of Midlothian* in 1830, the county of Fife is 'bounded by the two firths on the south and north, and by the sea on the east, and having a number of small seaports'. Indeed, it had picturesque villages with small harbours noted for their maritime life and fishing fleets in the time Horsburgh was born. Alexander Selkirk, a mariner who was marooned for several years on an uninhabited island whose story inspired Defoe to create his character Robinson Crusoe, was also born in this area just a few miles along the coast from Elie in Largo.

Horsburgh's studies at the local school came to an end at age 16 when, in common with many of his countrymen from that area, he went to sea. Initially, he was an ordinary seaman in ships plying coastal and European waters until 1780 when he was captured by the French and imprisoned in Dunkirk. His imprisonment was short lived and his further sea voyages thereafter took him to the East. It was on a journey from Batavia to Ceylon, following a chart which indicated they were in open water, that their ship foundered on the island of Diego Garcia. The experience encouraged him to examine charts critically and he resolved to make observations on his own sea journeys and improve their accuracy. As his maritime experience developed and his number of voyages increased, so did his detailed knowledge as he recorded data at sea and studied in his periods ashore. His work was brought to the attention of a fellow Scot, Alexander Dalrymple, the Hydrographer of the East India Company whose ships monopolised the British trade with the East at this time.

Much of Horsburgh's early charts and observations were simply sent on to Dalrymple and the company but, gaining confidence, he eventually published under his own name to considerable acclaim. His publication, *Directions for sailing to the East Indies, China, New Holland, the Cape of Good Hope and the Interjacent Ports*, if not snappily named, became the standard and essential reference work for mariners voyaging in these waters and thus opened the way for trade to all these eastern regions.

Horsburgh returned to the United Kingdom in 1805 and, on the death of Dalrymple in 1810, was appointed his successor as Hydrographer of the East India Company. He continued to refine his works and observations until his death in 1836 and became known as the nautical oracle of the world.

Without his pioneering efforts in charting the seas, its many obstacles and the long routes to the East, later journeys would have been considerably more hazardous. The dedication of the lighthouse at Pedra Branca in his name, commanding the eastern entrance to the Straits of Singapore – through which pass currently many hundreds of ships each day – is a fitting tribute and memorial to a man who made the seas safer for future generations of mariners and paved the way for the development of trade in Singapore and the wider region.

John Turnbull Thomson

The thirty-four metre high Horsburgh Lighthouse was completed in 1851 by John Turnbull Thomson who arrived in the Malay Straits in 1838 and was appointed Government Surveyor and Superintendent of Roads and Public Works in Singapore in 1844. Born of Scottish parents in the North of England in 1821, Thomson moved to Scotland where he was educated at Duns Academy, Marischal College, Aberdeen, and Edinburgh University before finalising his education in the north of England.

Duns is a small town in the eastern Scottish Borders just south of Edinburgh where, it is said, that the young Thomson mixed with the children of owners of large estates in Penang. This fired his imagination and enthusiasm for moving to the East. It is more than likely that these owners were the relatives of David Brown and James Scott, Scots from Longformacus, Berwickshire, in the Scottish Borders and the trading partners of Francis Light, the founder of Penang. Brown rose to become the largest landowner in Penang with nutmeg plantations and many business interests in the region. There is also a possibility that David Brown was a member of the same family as George Henry Brown, after whom the Bukit Brown in Singapore is named although as yet no direct connection has been established.

The proposal for a light at Pedra Branca was put forward by a group of merchants from Canton led by the Scottish doctor William Jardine. He decided to raise funds for a memorial to Horsburgh. No doubt, Jardine was aware of the debt he owed to hydrographers such as Horsburgh in easing the journey to the East through their charts. Jardine was in partnership with another Scot, Edinburgh University graduate James Matheson who together formed the formidable trading house of Jardine Matheson. Over 4,000 Straits dollars was raised by Jardine and passed over to the administrators of the Strait Settlements who, in turn, commissioned Thomson to proceed with the work on a lighthouse. The building started in 1849 and was completed two years later at a total cost of over 23,000 Straits dollars.

As surveyor, Thomson was responsible for much of the public infrastruc-

Overleaf: J T Thomson and three of his views showing Telok Blangah, Singapore town and Cathedral of the Good Shepherd. (University of Otago)

J. T. THOMSON,

Government Surveyor,

1846.

ture which made the growing colony of Singapore function effectively, from roads, bridges, various engineering works and hospitals. In 1852, his report on the Singapore water supply led to the construction of a reservoir initially named Thomson Reservoir and renamed MacRitchie Reservoir.

Thomson was also the architect and builder of the Tan Tock Seng Hospital, the second St Andrew's Cathedral, the Dalhousie Obelisk and the first bridge over the Kallang River known as Thomson Bridge as well as the graceful Hajjah Fatimah Mosque completed in 1846 on the site in Beach Road of the dwelling house of Hajjah Fatimah who left a sum of money for its construction. Thomson both designed and constructed the mosque in an eclectic mixture of Eastern and Western styles, lending a unique character to this building. It amply illustrates the point that the terms 'superintendent' and 'surveyor' are nowhere near adequate to describe the all-round talent of Thomson who could turn his hand both to robust and practical construction and elegant and artistic design.

In addition to these skills, he was an accomplished self-taught painter and writer of some note, having left many amusing commentaries on his travels in the East and Singapore. His painting of the Pedra Branca Lighthouse is an excellent record of its imposing construction, as are many of his works which give a clear and unique perspective of the early topography of Singapore.

Although the Pedra Branca Lighthouse is dedicated to the memory of Horsburgh and bears his name, it should perhaps also be regarded as an appropriate memorial to Thomson as it took two years of his life in what must have been a time of great privation that exerted a physical toll on his constitution such that he was invalided back home to Britain from where he was advised to seek more temperate climes.

Thomson then moved to New Zealand, arriving in Auckland in 1856, where his talents continued to flourish. In his major survey of Otago published in 1860, he named many mountains, rivers and other geographical features after places in his homeland in the North of England and Scotland, including one mountain named Earnslaw, the name of the farm of his grandfather James Thomson, near Coldstream in Berwickshire, Scotland.

On retirement, Thomson moved to Invercargill in New Zealand, where he would have no doubt been at home as many of the inhabitants were Scots emigres. Many of the streets in Invercargill bear the name of Scottish places and rivers including, the Don, Dee and Spey. He died there in 1884, his considerable talents having created a lasting legacy in both Singapore and New Zealand where his residence, which he designed, is now protected as a historic place. He is remembered in Singapore by Thomson Road, a major trunk artery linking the centre of the business district with the north of the city. He is also believed to be the *ang mo* (red haired person, Caucasian in Chinese dialect) referred to in the district of Ang Mo Kio – literally Red Hair Bridge – having built a bridge in the area.

The Dalhousie Obelisk

Dalhousie Castle, in the county of Midlothian, Scotland, is a mere eight miles to the south of the capital Edinburgh. The castle, built in the mid-18th century, overlooking the River North Esk in a picturesque setting, was the seat of the Earls of Dalhousie, chiefs of the clan Ramsay. James Andrew Broun Ramsay, the youngest son of the family in the early 19th century, inherited the peerage from his father who died in 1838, his two older brothers having predeceased him.

Educated privately at Harrow School and Christ Church, Oxford, he experienced a setback in contesting a parliamentary seat in Edinburgh; his accession to the peerage, however, offered him the opportunity to progress and he quickly rose to influence in Parliament in Britain, becoming Vice President of the Board of Trade in 1843 under Gladstone, the President. In 1845, he succeeded Gladstone as President of the Board of Trade and, in 1847, his rise continued when he was appointed Governor-General of India.

The Earl visited Singapore in February 1850 and an eye-witness account of his arrival is provided by a native of the Shetland Islands, to the north of the Scottish mainland, who wrote a 'Letter from Singapore' dated 23 February 1850, published in *The Shetland Times*, describing the scene. The unknown writer who signed himself 'A Singapore Zetlander', opened with the comment that he writes from the 'veritable city of Gutta Percha, Singapore.' He described the visit as follows: 'About half-past nine o'clock his lordship left the HC steamer, 'Feroze' and was pulled towards the river through a double row of the famous Singapore sampans – native boats of all but unequalled speed. The men-of-war in the roads had their yards manned, while the flags which they and a noble fleet of merchantmen were decorated, contrasted proudly with the grotesque ensigns of a crowd of native craft and Chinese junks.' He described the welcoming party, consisting of the Governor, the 'native chief' of the island 'supported by two handsome Malay youths – his sons – and attended by his sword-bearer,' and the senior traders; the carriage then passed through 'a group in their picturesque holiday costumes, consisting of respectable Chinese merchants, together with Armenians, Jews, Arabs, Parsees, Malays, Klings, Bugis, and others, exhibiting such a motley

band as perhaps no town in the world can produce, among a population like that of Singapore of 26,000 inhabitants.'

Our Singapore Zetlander comments on the Governor-General's 'bond of sympathy which his rank or power alone could never have elicited', and further refers to the 'soundness of his judgement and his peculiar fitness for the high post he adorns.' The feeling must have been shared by the other European immigrants who saw fit to mark the occasion of his visit with the construction of an obelisk and an inscription which echoes these sentiments. During his stay in Singapore the public receptions held in his honour were organised by James Guthrie of the major Scottish trading house bearing that name.

The Dalhousie Obelisk, its elegant design having been influenced by the famed Cleopatra's Needle standing on the embankment of the River Thames in London, now stands at Empress Place. It originally stood on a renamed Dalhousie Pier and moved as land was reclaimed. The obelisk was designed and constructed by John Turnbull Thomson and it would have been no surprise to the Governor-General to see a fellow Scot in such a distinguished position and to be involved in creating such a fitting tribute to mark the occasion of his visit.

Dalhousie served in India until 1856 when ill health forced a return home. He died at Dalhousie Castle in December 1860.

St Andrew's Cathedral

St Andrew's Cathedral is one of many prominent landmarks in Singapore which is strongly linked to Scots immigrants. The name is that of Scotland's Patron Saint. Although most Scots of the era would have, as a legacy of John Knox, been staunch presbyterians from the Church of Scotland, 'the kirk' as it was popularly known, the majority of contributors to the construction of this Anglican church were Scots and the name was chosen in recognition of their major financial contribution.

The story of how St Andrew became the Patron Saint of Scotland is steeped in myth and legend. Many years after his death by crucifixion by the Romans, the bones of St Andrew were taken by Constantine for protection and safekeeping. Later, one of his devotees and followers, St Regulus, had a vision which saw him taking the saint's bones to a far off land. Regulus fulfilled his vision by travelling north with the precious burden and eventually arrived in Scotland. The bones were laid to rest in the town now known as St Andrews. In advance of what was to become a decisive battle, prayers were offered and the clouds parted to form the shape of the St Andrew's cross in

The Dalhousie Obelisk at its original site at Dalhousie Pier (Private Collection) and James Andrew Broun Ramsay, Earl of Dalhousie.

the sky. The ensuing victory resulted in the symbol being adopted as the national flag and St Andrew as the Patron Saint of Scotland.

With the long Scottish history, many stories such as the ones above have accumulated, and in many instances the myths and legends which surround the history have become better known than the historical facts themselves. Celebrated in ballads, poetry and song they have developed into powerful emblems, which have created and underpinned the identity of Scotland and the Scottish people for centuries.

In Singapore, the first Church of St Andrew was designed by the Irishman George Drumgoole Coleman and was constructed around 1835 to 1836. This first building was enhanced with a tower and a spire designed and built by John Turnbull Thomson. This building suffered two damaging lightning strikes in 1845 and 1849 and was subsequently demolished. A second building was started in 1856 and completed in 1862. This final cathedral was built by Indian convict labour under the design of Singapore's Engineer and Superintendent of Convicts, Colonel Ronald MacPherson.

Lieutenant-Colonel Ronald MacPherson

Ronald MacPherson was born on the Isle of Skye on 14 July 1817. At that time, the island would have been almost entirely Gaelic speaking, and remains today a stronghold of Gaelic language and culture. Gaelic would certainly have been the first language of the young MacPherson, whose name in Gaelic would have been Mac a'Phearsain, meaning 'son of the parson'. The family name comes from Badenoch in the central area of Scotland where the name referred to one who was a steward of church property rather than a preacher.

MacPherson, like so many of his countrymen, became a soldier, enlisting initially in the East India Company military college before joining the Madras Artillery on his graduation in 1836 at the age of 19.

The East India Company, having been awarded the monopoly for British trade to the East Indies, had the need to protect, expand and defend its interests. From its foundation in 1600, it had soldiers for protection and, gradually, this effectively private army, was transformed into an effective and formidable fighting force of several regiments comprising over 300,000 soldiers by 1820.

Joining the Madras Artillery, MacPherson was sent to India where he learned Arabic and Hindustani, and studied engineering. He saw action in the Opium War of 1842 in China and, on cessation of hostilities, was posted to Penang where he was, after six years, appointed Engineer and Superinten-

Lt-Col Ronald MacPherson.

dent of Convicts. After a further six years in Penang, he was promoted to the same post on transfer to Singapore in 1855.

In addition to the successful completion of St Andrew's Cathedral, which received much acclaim for its elegance and design, MacPherson was responsible for the building of the Victoria Concert Hall, initially constructed as the Town Hall.

His interest in military matters were rekindled in his founding of the Singapore Volunteer Rifle Corps (SVRC) in July 1854, becoming its Commandant Captain, in response to secret society riots involving Teochew and Hokkien groups in May of that year when up to 400 people were killed and 300 houses burned down.

The SVRC had an illustrious history. Initially funded privately by the participants themselves, it was taken over by the Government in 1857. It was disbanded briefly in December 1887 but reformed in February 1888 as the Singapore Volunteer Artillery becoming, in 1901, the Singapore Volunteer Corps which was in action in the First World War. In 1922 it became the Straits Settlements Volunteer Force and was involved in action against the Japanese in the defence of Singapore during the Second World War.

By 1939, the SSVF numbered four infantry battalions which drew its members from Singapore (1st and 2nd battalions), Malacca (4th) and Penang (3rd). The battalions were segregated racially into companies and, in addition to having Eurasian, English, Chinese and Malay companies, had sufficient Scots to have C company entirely Scottish. In 1954, the force was merged with the Singapore armed services and was active during the Malayan Emergency. With Singapore's independence in 1965, the volunteer corps was renamed the Peoples' Defence Force.

MacPherson moved to Malacca as Resident Councillor in 1858 and his success there and before led to a number of other sensitive appointments including advising Raja Juma'at of Lukut before returning to Singapore in 1860 as Resident Councillor.

In 1867, the Straits Settlements were transferred from direct control by India to the British Colonial Office. The transfer proceeded without difficulty for which the Governor Sir Harry Ord credited Macpherson.

Macpherson died suddenly in Singapore on 6 December 1869. He is remembered by a memorial in the grounds of St Andrew's Cathedral and in MacPherson Road. Perhaps as a Scottish soldier, he would have been most proud of his legacy in pioneering a voluntary military movement, the spirit of which lives on in the Singapore Armed Forces Volunteer Corp established in 2015.

James MacRitchie

Singapore in 1823, as a growing trading post, required fresh water and the Resident John Crawfurd proposed the construction of waterworks and a reservoir. This proposal, however, came to nothing presumably because of lack of funds and the demand of even more urgent works to ensure the development of the new settlement.

By 1857, things must have been desperate and Straits Chinese trader, businessman and philanthropist Tan Kim Seng donated the sum of $13,000 towards the cost of the necessary works. However, the sum required was $100,000 and construction was delayed again. It was not until 1868 that a reservoir was completed and, even then, it did not have the distribution and pumping mechanisms in place until 1877.

Tan Kim Seng had died in 1864, and the government, suitably embarrassed at the poor progress and some botched decisions in this area, decided in 1882 to honour and recognise Mr Tan's generous contribution with the installation of a fountain at Fullerton Square. Like so many landmarks the fountain has been moved to suit progress and later construction works and now proudly stands in Esplanade Park in memory of Mr Tan.

The original reservoir was constructed under the supervision of the engineer John Turnbull Thomson and it was known variously as the Impounding Reservoir and Thomson Reservoir. In 1891, the holding capacity of the reservoir was increased significantly at a cost of $32,000. There were considerable losses due to leaks from the holding and piping systems and the findings led to a scheme to enlarge the reservoir to 650 million gallons as well as to make improvements to purification and pumping systems. All these works were approved and implemented by James MacRitchie by the end of 1894.

James MacRitchie was an engineer born in Southampton, England, to Scottish parents. His father Alexander MacRitchie of Greenock, Scotland, was Superintendent Engineer of the Peninsular and Oriental Steam Navigation Company, a major shipping line, many of whose steamers would have commenced their journey and plied the Atlantic and Orient routes from a base in Southampton.

James was sent to Scotland for his education and was schooled in Dollar Institution, now known as Dollar Academy, in Crieff, founded in 1818 from a legacy of the successful merchant Captain John Mcnabb, and at Edinburgh University. He then undertook an apprenticeship in the Glasgow engineering company Bell and Miller working on docks, harbours and slipways as well as a number of bridges in and around Glasgow.

JAMES MACRITCHIE M. INST. C. E.
MUNICIPAL ENGINEER OF SINGAPORE
1883 — 1895

Following appointments which took him to China, Japan and Brazil, MacRitchie was appointed Municipal Engineer of Singapore in May 1883, a post which he took up in September of that year and held until his death in April 1895.

During those 12 years, his efforts produced much of the infrastructure which the city benefits from today. Bridges, abattoirs, water systems and markets were all constructed during his term of office. Excellent and durable roadways were laid down as well as a number of bridges constructed. On his arrival in Singapore there were two iron bridges of satisfactory quality and twenty-three when he departed.

He arranged for improvement to markets, in particular the Telok Ayer Market structure. He had some difficulty in relation to the construction and commissioning of new abattoirs since there were a number of cultural prejudices and taboos to be negotiated; this he did with skill and diplomacy. His efforts extended also to solutions for the disposal of sewage, which in a relatively flat island, were not obvious; he found inspiration by examining the sanitation in some of the chief towns in India and Burma.

When he arrived in Singapore, the population was about 100,000 with a water consumption of 1,400,000 gallons a day; on his death, the population had increased to 145,000 and water consumption 3,400,000 gallons.

The legacy and the name of the engineer responsible has been recognised and preserved in the name of the MacRitchie Reservoir. A much loved area for recreation and forest reserve, it is a fitting tribute to perseverance, engineering skill and determination.

MacRitchie Reservoir is also a place where we can witness some of the finest ironwork in Singapore which was made in Scotland. The shelters housing the sluice mechanisms which project out into the water, are both practical and elegant; each pillar supporting the canopy bears the makers mark of the MacFarlane foundry in Glasgow.

The Cavenagh Bridge

Opened in 1870, the Cavenagh Bridge spans the Singapore River. This classically stylish but practical bridge was, like many iron structures in Singapore, built in Glasgow by iron founders and shipped out for assembly by convict workers.

The Cavenagh Bridge was constructed by P & W MacLellan of Glasgow. MacLellan was one of many iron companies operating in and around the west of Scotland in the 19th century. Starting off as a hardware store in Glasgow in 1805, it progressed gradually through a series of partnerships

MacRitchie Reservoir and the memorial plaque of James MacRitchie.

supplying a variety of ironmongery services and goods. In 1846, they added iron merchanting to their product line and, two years later, started making iron bridges. Their first bridge, completed in 1852, crossed the River Clyde in Glasgow. MacLellan expanded their business into the teak trade through links to companies operating in Burma, where Scots were also well represented, and gave them a near monopoly for this natural resource used mainly for construction of piers and harbours.

MacLellan were also known as the Clutha Iron Works, Clutha being an old name for the Clyde. It is said that the Clyde made Glasgow but Glasgow made the Clyde. This refers to the fact that, initially, the river was not navigable very far upstream and, after being dredged, managed to allow shipbuilding to be done further upstream and also to allow Glasgow to successfully develop as a port and claim the honour of the 'second city' of the Empire for many years.

The Cavenagh Bridge, which links the business and civic districts, was built at a cost of $80,000 under the order of John Turnbull Thomson, Government Surveyor and Superintendent of Roads and Public Works. Designing and buying a bridge, having it shipped across thousands of miles of ocean and then arranging for it to be assembled is not a normal day's work. The combination of confidence, vision and skill at both Singapore and in Glasgow, together with the individual efforts of workers to manufacture to closely defined tolerances and measurement in the absence of knowledge of the site, terrain and underlying ground conditions is nothing short of astonishing. In days when communication took many months, the requirement that the information sent had to be precise and had to be right first time is something which appears to have no modern day equivalent. The bridge stands today, still in prime condition, almost 150 years later as testament to that vision and skill.

Workers in the Industrial Revolution in Britain had a life expectancy of just over 40 years. Hours were long with unrelenting hard labour in an atmosphere of noise, dust and ever present danger from unguarded machinery, molten metal, movement of materials and mistakes made by exhausted people. We don't hear much of the stories of those who did the work, only the names of those in charge.

A review of the Scottish Census of 1851, which records the occupation of the respondents, reveals many iron founders. Some of those might have worked for MacLellan's on the construction of this bridge:

William Muir, aged 20, iron founder – born Lanarkshire, living with his father who was a ploughman, his mother and three siblings.

James Napier, aged 23, iron founder – born Renfrewshire, living with his parents, his father was a labourer, and six siblings.

Michael Pambudge, iron founder, aged 15, born Ayrshire living with his father, also listed as an iron founder, his mother and four siblings.

Robert Ereskine, aged 59, iron founder, living with a nephew, aged 16, an apprentice iron founder.

The Factory Act of 1819, the same year as the 'founding' of Singapore, limited the work of children in Britain to less than twelve hours a day; the 1833 Factory Act improved the situation slightly by banning workers younger than 9 years old and limiting the hours of those aged 10 to 13 to a 48 hour week. We can only speculate on the lives of those who worked in iron foundries and the miners who hewed coal to fire them but their product graced, embellished and eased the burden of many in Britain's trading posts across the globe.

The bridge across the Singapore River built in 1868 was planned initially to be named after the Duke of Edinburgh, whose name is recognised in Edinburgh Road in the Istana grounds – the former colonial Government House – and in its Edinburgh Gate entrance. Although they bear the name of the capital of Scotland they have no direct connection with Scotland itself, it being merely an honorific title conferred by the monarch as and when he or she determines. The title is currently held by Prince Philip consort to Queen Elizabeth.

Still, the name Edinburgh Bridge was fitting as the genesis of the project was from the mind of a Scots engineer and it was manufactured in Glasgow, and no doubt shipped out to Singapore in a ship built on the River Clyde.

But the bridge was eventually named after Sir William Orfeur Cavenagh, the last Governor of the Straits Settlements appointed by India who governed from 1859 to 1867.

The Cavenagh Bridge of course would have been regarded as small beer by MacLellan which was dealing with the likes of Indian Railways, where contracts for almost 50 bridges at a time were not unusual, as well as major contracts at home for bridges across the rivers Forth and Tay. Clearly, the business of empire was profitable for business owners and investors. The business in 1890 was one of Scotland's major companies with over 3,000 employees. It has continued under various names to the present day but as a much smaller organisation and specialising in a different product range. Singapore's link with MacLellan was renewed in recent times through the frequent visits to Singapore's Nanyang Technical University of the late Professor Douglas MacLellan, a direct descendant of the founder of the firm,

Overleaf: William Orfeur Cavenagh and Cavenagh Bridge, 1900. (Private Collection)

who had a distinguished career as an academic engineer.

Ornamental ironwork, bringing together the airy fretwork of seaside frivolity and the solidity and weight of national strength, has been used to embellish cities for many centuries to commemorate events and display civic pride and wealth. These take the form of fountains, railings, ornamental gates, bandstands and verandahs of all descriptions.

Strolling in a park with the strains of music hall tunes or military marches drifting from a cast iron bandstand, or striding along a seaside iron constructed pier or promenade with Punch and Judy shows and fairground attractions, quenching thirst with a drink of clean water from a newly installed fountain, all would be a pleasurable escape from the drudgery of factory life for the fortunate few who had time off on a Sunday. Such was the memory that perhaps prompted early settlers to import such items to Singapore. The re-creation of home would no doubt be a preoccupation for some.

The Victorian and Edwardian eras in Britain were devoted to ironwork street furniture and its use in architectural ornamentation: a reflection of the pride in empire and a celebration of the money it was making. Town halls across Britain built in the Victorian period display the wealth being brought back from empire success. Glasgow City Chambers is a prime example; completed in 1888, its imposing frontage looms over the city centre, dominating the east side of George Square. Its interior of marbled halls, sweeping staircases, a vast banqueting hall, domes and cupolas, was designed to impress and speak of the glories of supplying the Empire with ships and engineering, and trading in and manufacture of tobacco and sugar.

MacFarlane and Company was a premier producer of ornamental ironwork in Scotland during the 19th century. Founded in 1850 by Walter MacFarlane in Glasgow, the foundry area, by 1890, extended to 14 acres and had swollen the local population by 10,000. The pollution was legendary. Its principal products included drinking fountains, bandstands, railings, lamp standards and architectural ornamentation. Like MacLellan, its business interests spread far beyond the confines of Glasgow and Scotland. The Empire was its customer base and it provided a steady supply of the items listed as civic pride burgeoned in growing trading posts and colonies.

Singapore was no exception. MacFarlane provided a wide range of items which decorate the city to this day. The elegant railings round the Singapore Parliament on High Street and North Boat Quay conform to a MacFarlane design and are almost certainly one of their products made at the Saracen Foundry.

The ironwork of the entrance canopy to Raffles Hotel was supplied by

MacFarlane and although much of the original work was removed during the war, replicas have been carefully made during 1989 refurbishment of the hotel. Original drawings from MacFarlane and some photographs were used to recreate the works. The elegant drinking fountain currently in the court-yards of Raffles Hotel was built by MacFarlane and was originally placed from 1902 until the 1930s in front of Orchard Road Market.

The Telok Ayer Market (or Lau Pa Sat) in the Singapore business district attracts a lunchtime bustling crowd from nearby banks, finance houses and trading company headquarters, with many diners unaware of the illustrious history of the elegant building which shelters them from the midday sun.

The first market was on the south side of the Singapore River but moved when developments suggested better use could be made of that space. In 1825, the market was moved to Telok Ayer Street where produce could be loaded directly from the waterfront. James MacRitchie the engineer, influenced by Coleman's earlier design, designed the current building in 1894 and arranged for its construction in cast iron by MacFarlane in Glasgow.

The beauty, simplicity and classical elegance of the current Lau Pa Sat, fully restored and refurbished in the 1980s, stands in stark contrast to the surrounding brash concrete, glass and steel. The juxtaposition, however, emphasises the past and present strengths of Singapore; the marketplace as a

Raffles Hotel with its ironwork canopy, c 1913. (Private Collection)

symbol of its history and a legacy of its strategic position on the sea lanes between China and India; today's finance houses and industry headquarters less tangibly but no less effectively, linked to the world's networks by wireless technology, transferring funds and commodities with the press of a button rather than the sweat of a thousand coolies, stevedores, mariners and harbourmasters.

There are many more examples of Scottish ironwork in Singapore. Indeed, with the absence of any iron and steel works in the region, it is probable that most of such works were imported from Scotland where the major manufacturing was based. Railings around the Maghain Aboth Synagogue in Waterloo Street bear the maker's mark of the Sun Foundry in Glasgow and the interior of the Chesed-El Synagogue in Oxley Rise boasts fine ironwork by MacFarlane. The building was constructed by the Scottish Engineering and Architectural firm of Swan & Maclaren, who must have made use of their Scottish contacts when designing the interior.

A key element of a synagogue is the Ark, built to face west towards Jerusalem, and placed on a raised platform surrounded by a lattice work of iron railing. Edmund Lim WK and Kho Ee Moi in their *The Chesed-El Synagogue: Its History and People* stated that during a major refurbishment in 2001, 'new lattice iron railings surrounding the platform were manufactured by the same company in Scotland that made the original railings for the synagogue more than ninety-five years ago'. They continue: 'The trustees also decided to replace the timber balustrade with a copy of the original cast iron railings'. The originals had been made by Walter MacFarlane and Company and its successor company Heritage Engineering of Glasgow was able to recreate the railings.

The balconies at the Singapore Cricket Club, installed in 1884, conform to designs of MacFarlane and although the Anderson Bridge has no maker's mark, it is characteristic of MacFarlane's work.

Singapore is fortunate to have such a legacy of ironwork from the late 19th century and should celebrate its survival. There was a huge quantity of railings, gates and ironwork throughout Britain but much of it was destroyed during the Second World War. This was not havoc wrought by enemy bombers but the deliberate destruction of vast quantities of ornamental iron for munitions. There are few examples remaining of railings, except those which were retained as barriers to hazardous features; those for purely ornamental purpose were removed to support the war effort.

Each railing, parapet, fountain or architectural embellishment is a testament to those who had the vision to see the need for a work of elegance rather than one of pure utility, to those men that toiled in the heat, hot blast and dust and danger of dark foundries, the shippers and those who hoisted the precious and weighty burdens from the banks of the Singapore River and the labourers, often pressed or prisoners, who toiled in the heat and humidity to assemble the puzzle of ironwork. The works themselves stand as a silent memorial to them all rather than to the grandees immortalised by names emblazoned on escutcheons.

Architecture
One of the most influential Scottish firms in terms of creating the Singapore cityscape is Swan & Maclaren. Archibald Alexander Swan and James Waddell Boyd Maclaren were both Scottish engineers. Initially formed as Swan & Lermit in 1887, Lermit left the partnership in 1890 and worked for another firm, Crane & Co, before setting up on his own on 1 March 1897 in practice as Architect and Surveyor. The new partnership of Swan & Maclaren was formed in 1890 on Lermit's departure.

Swan, born in the Maryhill district in the north of Glasgow on 6 February 1857, was awarded a BSc from Glasgow University in 1877, and became a member of the Institution of Civil Engineers in 1885. Maclaren was born in Edinburgh on 14 April 1863, into a family which hailed from Moffatt in the Scottish Borders and, like Swan, became a civil engineer, being admitted to membership of the Institution of Civil Engineers in March 1898.

The partnership of Swan & Maclaren was engaged in a diverse range of engineering, surveying and architectural work typical of a fast developing economy; responsible for railways, goldfield surveys, roads, piers and work throughout the Malayan peninsula and beyond. There was also a connection with oilfield development and copper mines and Swan was Chairman of the Caucasus Copper Company founded in 1901.

In Singapore, their legacy is a contribution to a grand cityscape of landmark buildings including Raffles Hotel in 1889, Stamford House and the Teutonia Club (now Goodwood Park Hotel) in 1900, the Adelphi Hotel in 1904, the Chesed-El Synagogue in 1905, the John Little building in Raffles Place in 1907, as well as the various incarnations of St Joseph's Church in 1906, 1938 and 1956. The architectural genius behind most of these was the Englishman, Regent Alfred John Bidwell who was joined in 1907 by the Scot, David Macleod Craik. Craik's childhood was passed in the Stewartry in south-west Scotland, not far from Moffatt, and it is possible that he was a family friend of the Maclaren's.

Craik, born in 1873, joined the firm in 1913 shortly before the First

Singapore, Teutonia Club.

JOHN LITTLE @ RAFFLES PLACE

ADELPHI HOTEL
BAR AND BILLIARD ROOM

ESTABLISHED 1863

Adelphi Hotel
Singapore

World War started. As he was due home leave, he returned to Britain and was called up for military service. Although wounded, he survived the war and was demobbed in 1919 as a captain in the Royal Engineers. Craik returned to Singapore and shortly afterwards opened up the Swan & Maclaren practice in Penang. He was an active member of the community, a secretary of the Tanglin Club and, for many years, a member of the St Andrew's Society where he organised the annual ball. He died in 1938. Maclaren died sadly at the young age of 47 in 1910 and Swan the year after in Glasgow at the age of 54.

Both Neoclassical and Palladian design and architecture were in evidence throughout the British Empire, influenced strongly by the fashionable success in Britain of the Scottish architects Robert Adam and Colin Campbell. Adam's work, in turn, was informed by his training in Rome which was prompted by his travels whilst undertaking the traditional 'grand tour' of Europe. Like Adam Smith, the renowned political economist, Robert Adam was born in Kirkcaldy, Fife, Scotland and educated at the Royal High School of Edinburgh. His designs, which became the most fashionable in Europe, remain an enduring influence on western architecture and that of the British Empire.

Scottish merchants were active in commissioning buildings of architectural merit in Singapore, one of the most significant being a Palladian mansion on a prominent part of the bank of the Singapore River, designed by Irish architect George Drumgoole Coleman for Scottish trader and Singapore magistrate John Argyle Maxwell. Maxwell, whose main business and estates were in Java, must have been both wealthy and influential to have commissioned such a mansion situated on the historic site where Farquhar and Raffles stepped ashore in Singapore in 1819. It was the Resident Crawfurd who gave the permission for the use of this prime location, but according to Jane Beamish and Jane Ferguson in their *History of Singapore Architecture, The Making of a City*, the next Resident questioned this and the matter was referred to Calcutta for resolution. The authorities in India were sanguine about the matter since work had already been completed at considerable expense to the owner and they resolved things by saying Maxwell could have the land but on a 999 year lease.

Maxwell came to Singapore in 1822 and stayed until 1828. His business interests involved extensive travel and he never was able to enjoy the significant house which he had financed. He leased it back to the government for 500 rupees and, after much alteration, was used as the Singapore Court and thereafter Singapore Parliament House.

From bottom: Adelphi Hotel (National Archives of Singapore), Teutonia Club and John Little. Overleaf: John Maxwell's house. (Private Collection)

J A Maxwell's business interests covered most of the East and he was one of the witnesses at the House of Commons Select Committee hearings into the business of the East India Company in March 1830. The details of the hearing give some fascinating detail about the trades he was making which included importing woollen clothes from Hamburg, Germany into Singapore which were then shipped to Canton under an American-flagged ship and bartered for black tea.

Death is the common denominator for all and one of the best ways of seeking out the past is from the tombstones in old cemeteries. The book *Spaces of the Dead*, edited by Kevin Tan, provides some interesting information on Scottish architect William Campbell Oman who began his career in Singapore in the Public Works Department in 1907. He was responsible for the design of a number of important buildings in Singapore principally the Moulmein Road Infectious Diseases Hospital (now Middleton Hospital) and the Salt Water Pumping Station.

The book also comments, 'Another Scotsman, Alexander Gordon FRIBA (died 29 April 1931 aged 38), was the Municipal Architect. Together with his assistant Frank D Meadows, he was responsible for the neo-Classical Municipal Building (later City Hall) and now part of the National Art Gallery complex. He served as Captain of the Scottish Company of the Singapore Volunteer Corps as well as President of the Institute of Architects of Malaya'. Following service in the First World War, Alexander Gordon returned to his studies at Architectural School in Aberdeen and, after qualifying as an architect, took up a post of Assistant Municipal Architect in Singapore in 1923 and was appointed Municipal Architect in 1925. Sadly, like so many of his compatriots, he did not make it back to his home country and died in Colombo on his way back to his home town of Aberdeen.

James Milner Fraser was born on 5 January 1905, the son of an ironmonger in Aberdeen. He completed his architectural apprenticeship in 1925 at the Aberdeen School of Architecture. After undertaking municipal work in London and a study tour of Rome, Florence and Paris, he emigrated in 1927 to Singapore where he joined the Singapore Improvement Trust working under his fellow Scot, Alexander Gordon. By the mid 1940s, he had been promoted to Manager to the Trust and, in ensuing years, supervised a number of major developments including more than 10,000 flats, shops and houses as well as writing papers on town planning issues. He died in Aberdeenshire in 1978.

The Singapore Improvement Trust was proposed in 1920 but it was not until 1927, the year Fraser joined, that it became formally constituted. The first major project of the new Trust was the Tiong Bahru Estate in the 1930s. Singapore Improvement Trust is regarded as the first public housing body in Singapore and was replaced on its dissolution in 1960 by the Housing Development Board.

In addition to the tangible legacy of bricks and mortar, Fraser also left an intangible memorial which is arguably more important and durable. The Boys' Brigade was founded in Glasgow in 1883 by Sir William Alexander Smith and has since spread to many countries of the world to give moral guidance and purpose to young boys and men. A company of BB had been established in China in the city of Swatow until it was forced to close because of persecution. A former Swatow BB member, Quek Eng Moh, recognized James Fraser as a fellow BB from his buttonhole badge and together they founded the First Singapore Company of BB at Prinsep Street Presbyterian Church on 12 January 1930. The company quickly rose to 30 members in 1930 and was over 200 by 1936. Fraser, who served as President from 1936 to 1956, was imprisoned by the Japanese during the war and worked on the infamous Burma Railroad. During the war, the Singapore BB colours were burned to prevent them falling into the hands of the Japanese but the drums were hidden in the Prinsep Street Church and recovered after the war.

The Boys' Brigade continues to thrive in Singapore to this day and Fraser is recognized as their founder in their current premises where the Fraser Hall is graced with a plaque confirming his contribution. His legacy as a Scot includes the formation of many pipe bands which again continue to this day in Singapore.

Other Scottish architects who made significant contributions to a growing Singapore in the 20th century include James Scott, born in 1897 in the parish of Rothes, north west of Aberdeen, who, like Gordon, emigrated to Singapore in 1925 to take up a post as assistant architect to the Municipal Commissioners. William Irving Watson was City Architect and Building Surveyor of Singapore in the early 1950s and on his move to private practice was succeeded by James Nisbet Lockerbie who returned to Edinburgh on his retirement in 1974.

James Kirkwood, born in Fairlie, Ayrshire, Scotland in 1917, had his studies interrupted by the Second World War where he reached the rank of Major, RSF Infantry. In 1949, he moved to Singapore as senior assistant in Palmer & Turner Architects, and was in-charge of a number of important projects including Crosby House, the Commercial Union Assurance Building, the American International Assurance Building and a number of telephone exchanges. He retired in the 1970s.

Place Names

A reliable commentary on the pioneers of any city or place can be found in the names of geographical features, streets, bridges and harbours. Local names, even if in use for centuries, would be discarded thoughtlessly as European settlers in the main, set about with presumptuous enthusiasm naming everything in sight with little regard for history or cultural sensitivities other than their own.

This pattern was applied where Scottish people settled and there are many Scottish cities, glens and rivers which have namesakes across the globe. There are many Edinburghs, including one city in New Zealand which took the old name for Edinburgh, Dunedin, and the city of Perth in Western Australia named after Perth in Scotland at the request of Britain's Secretary of State for the Colonies, Sir George Murray, who happened to be the Member of Parliament for Perthshire. There are known to be 16 Aberdeens, 19 Dundees, 10 Edinburghs as well as two Glencoes and several Ben Lomonds around the world. However, the Lanarkshire town of Hamilton, which in the 19th century was at the industrial heart of Scotland's heavy industries, takes the crown with no less than 75 namesakes.

In Singapore, roads named in the 19th century which have survived until today, record the names of early settlers, Asian and European, who owned land, provided valuable service, or who the local dignitaries simply felt should be recognised by a permanent memorial.

Looking at the names of streets in central Singapore we are faced with a cornucopia of Scottish names, Many might not realise the origin of the street names but in the older parts of the central area of the city a significant proportion are Scottish or of Scottish origin. Angus, Campbell, Erskine, Ardmore, Elgin, Dunearn, Dundee and more, all read like a Scottish Gazetteer.

Most names commemorate individuals but some appear to be chosen simply because whoever owned the estate liked the sound of the words or perhaps had visited the area in Scotland. There appears to be no particular reason for an estate in Siglap, for example, to bear the names of places from mainly the Scottish Borders in the same way a neighbouring estate owner must have enjoyed opera, where roads are tunefully named Figaro, Tosca, Carmen, Aida and others. Most names however, were purposeful and named after individuals who had contributed in some way to the early success of the settlement, rendered exemplary service or gained fame or fortune in some other part of the British Empire.

Haig Road in Singapore is named after Field Marshall Earl Haig, the distinguished commander of British forces in the First World War in northern

James Bruce, Lord Elgin and the original wrought-iron Elgin Bridge.

North Bridge Road, Singapore

BRITONS

"WANTS
YOU

JOIN YOUR COUNTRY'S ARMY
GOD SAVE THE KING

Reproduced by permission of LONDON OPINION

mainland Europe. The naming is no doubt in celebration of the allied victory in 1918, and little to do with the fact that Douglas Haig was a Scot, born in the calm grey surroundings of Charlotte Square, the architectural piece de resistance of James Craig's 18th century New Town design in Edinburgh. His family was the Haig of Haig's Scotch Whisky, the distillers famed for their 'Dimple' brand and the memorable advertising slogan, 'Don't be vague, ask for Haig.'

A number of other roads in Singapore commemorate the First World War with Foch and Allenby also represented. Haig was a controversial figure during the war, as wave after wave of men failed to return after being sent 'over the top' of the trenches; many reviled him as a butcher responsible for the massacre of troops at bloody battles such as the Somme and Passchendaele where he seemed incapable of altering old-fashioned tactics which gained little or no ground. Over 60,000 men died or were wounded on the first day of the Battle of the Somme alone, with over 600,000 lives being lost over the course of that single battle, a waste unparalleled in the history of warfare.

In Wade Davis's book, *Into the Silence*, he refers to the contrasting life of the staff officers, often billeted in sumptuous French chateaux and the men actually drowning in the mud of the trenches. Wade Davis highlights the insensitivity and lack of understanding of what was really going on when he recounts the remark Haig makes to his senior liaison officer, 'Have we really lost half a million men?' Wade Davis adds an observation of Haig from an officer, Charles Kenneth Howard-Bury, captured during the war, which neatly illustrates the different approach of the opposing sides, 'As he was escorted to the rear, he was astonished to see German staff officers close to the front, orchestrating the attacks'.

However, many regarded Douglas Haig as a saviour who won a war of attrition over stronger German forces and a grateful nation presented him an earldom in 1919, a gift of 100,000 pounds sterling and the estate of Bemersyde in the Scottish Borders. His enjoyment of the fruits of his wartime effort was not long lived and came to a premature end when he died of a heart attack in 1928. He was given a state funeral and is buried in Dryburgh Abbey in the Scottish Borders.

Another famed Field Marshall of the Empire and First War was Lord Horatio Herbert Kitchener. He was born in Ireland but died in Scotland. His face became one of the best known in Britain and abroad when his generously moustached visage glared out of a wartime recruiting poster declaring 'Join your country's army!' with an accusing finger pointing directly from the frame at all passersby.

Lord Kitchener in a British Army recruitment poster, 1914.

Like Haig, he had served time in the Empire, Africa and India principally, but it was on board ship travelling from the Scottish Orkney Islands to Russia on a diplomatic mission that in a force nine gale, his ship, just to the west of the Orkneys, struck a mine placed by a German U-Boat. Of the crew of 655 officers and men, only 12 survived the explosion and freezing waters. There is a very substantial and imposing memorial to Kitchener on Marwick Head, Orkney, on top of the impressive 600 foot cliffs which plunge steeply down to the sea where raucous seabirds scream, wheel and dive into wild and dark, icy waters.

Kitchener Road, which runs between Serangoon Road and Jalan Besar in the vibrant and colourful Little India district of Singapore is named in recognition of his service to the United Kingdom.

MacDonald House in Singapore is a distinctive landmark building at the end of Orchard Road and close to Bras Basah Road. Completed in 1949 and unusually faced in red brick, it was gazetted as a national monument in 2003. The building is named after Malcolm MacDonald, born in 1901 in Lossiemouth in the north-east of Scotland, a town now well known as a major operational base for the Royal Air Force. MacDonald was the second son of James Ramsay MacDonald who was Britain's first Labour Prime Minister.

He became a Member of Parliament himself in 1929 and quickly rose to high positions related to the Dominions and future Commonwealth countries. He was appointed Dominions Secretary in 1935 and was a minister in Churchill's wartime Government in 1940. His political career culminated with his appointment as Governor General of Malaya after which the title was altered to Commissioner General for the United Kingdom in South East Asia. It was in this capacity that he formally opened the building in 1949 which took his name. MacDonald was known to be of a liberal persuasion and distanced himself from the snobbish attitude of many expatriate British and he mixed openly with Asian races.

MacDonald House is notorious for its place in the 'Confrontation' between Indonesia, fearing a neo-colonialist plot, and Malaysia shortly after Singapore's accession to that new Federation; a status which persisted from 1963 until 1966. Two Indonesian marines placed a bomb on the mezzanine floor near a lift and caused extensive destruction. Windows were shattered and nearby vehicles were damaged. Throughout the confrontation a number of bombs were placed in Singapore but this was the single worst incident. Indonesia has recently reopened the wound caused by this incident by naming a warship after the two marines who perpetrated this atrocity. The building remains to this day housing a bank and a number of commercial tenants.

Many roads bear the names of influential Scots of their day. The following are illustrative of some of the major characters whose memories have been preserved in street and place names.

Adam Road, named after Frank Adam, a former Managing Director of Pulau Brani Tin Smelting Works and President of the St Andrew's Society for five years.

Anderson Bridge and Anderson Street named after Sir John Anderson, Governor of the Straits Settlements from 1904 to 1907. Sir John was born in Aberdeen in 1858. His father, also John, was the Superintendent of the Gordon Mission, an evangelical Christian organisation. After graduating from Aberdeen University with a first class degree in mathematics and the gold medal for his class, the younger Anderson enlisted to the Colonial Service. In 1901, he was chosen to accompany the Duke and Duchess of York on a world tour of the British colonies and he would have had his first sight of Singapore on this prestigious voyage. Shortly after, in 1904, he was appointed Governor of the Straits Settlements, a position he held until 1911 when he was appointed Governor of Ceylon. He died suddenly in Ceylon in 1918.

Campbell Lane is named after Robert Campbell, a partner in the trading company Martin Dyce & Co.

One of the most sought after pieces of real estate in modern Singapore must be the site on the corner of Orchard Road and Scott's Road, stretching back to that one time haunt and watering hole of well heeled colonials, the Tanglin Club. This was the estate of Captain William George Scott, a major Singapore landowner who claimed to be a first cousin of the writer Sir Walter Scott. The picturesque and pleasing gardens of Scott's estate, a popular place for local residents to gather and enjoy the cool of the evening quiet tropical air scented with the fragrance of exotic fruits and spices, are a far cry from the fumes of today's metropolis, upmarket malls, jostling shoppers and smart hotels.

Captain Scott, who was also the Harbour Master and Post Master in Singapore, gives his name to Scott's Road while Claymore Road takes its name from the name of his house and estate. Claymore is an anglicisation of the Gaelic *claidheamh mor* meaning broad sword. Captain William G Scott was born in 1786. His father was James Scott born in Longformacus in the Scottish Borders and one of the people working in the East who inspired the young John Turnbull Thompson to come to Singapore. James Scott was the business partner of Francis Light, the founder of Penang, and David Brown, one of the largest landowners in that area. Captain William Scott's Claymore Plantation was one of the largest in Singapore and cultivated sea cotton and cocoa as well as a wide variety of fruits including rambutan, mangosteen and durian. In addition, he had a nutmeg plantation, also of considerable size, with over 5,000 trees. Scott was an active member of the Freemasons. He died in December 1861.

Scott's residence was a small, attap-roofed dwelling called Hurricane Cottage. This must have been replaced at some point by a much grander residence known as Hurricane House. When the young Thai King Chulalongkorn visited Singapore in 1871 he was very much taken by it and decided to purchase the property which eventually became the site of the Royal Thai Embassy in Singapore. In celebration of his visit, King Chulalongkorn presented Singapore a handsome bronze statue of an elephant which now stands outside the former mansion built by John Argyle Maxwell which in turn became Parliament House and is now The Arts House. Scott's property was acquired by the young Thai King with the aid of Tan Kim Ching, one of the sons of Tan Tock Seng, Singapore's famous Chinese pioneer businessman and philanthropist.

It was also Tan Kim Ching, on a suggestion from William Adamson of Adamson & Gilfillan, later the Borneo Company Limited, who recommended a young widow, Anna Leonowens to the Thai royal family as a tutor. This story became widely known through the film and musical *The King and I*. The impoverished Anna was living in Singapore with two young children after being widowed in Penang. Her daughter Avis later married a Scottish banker, Thomas Fyshe, and ended their financial worries whilst the son Louis returned to Thailand and joined the cavalry.

Dr J C Cumming, after whom Cumming Street is named, had connections with Freemasonry and was likely a Scot by virtue of the surname as indeed is Ellis who also has a road named after him. No existant records are available on these personalities.

Elgin Bridge is one of the principal crossings of the Singapore River carrying heavy traffic linking the main arteries of North and South Bridge Roads. The first bridge on this site, erected in 1863, was named Thomson Bridge after J T Thomson. However, it was renamed after yet another Scot, James Bruce, the 8th Earl of Elgin and 12th Earl of Kincardine. Elgin is a country town situated in the north-east of Scotland and Kincardine is an old county name from just to the south of this. It was Kincardineshire that Major General William Farquhar hailed from.

The smallest city in Scotland, nestling close to the River Spey, Elgin boasts a 13th century cathedral and is famed for its whisky distilleries with seven within easy reach of the city centre.

Top right: Sir John Anderson. Bottom right: Anderson Bridge, c 1920s.

Lord Elgin's father, the 7th Earl of Elgin, a renowned Scottish nobleman and diplomat, is notorious for his part in his controversial purchase of the famed 'marbles' from the Parthenon in Athens. He later sold them to the British Museum in London where the 'Elgin Marbles' are beautifully displayed to great acclaim. His son James also had a distinguished diplomatic career, culminating in his appointment as Viceroy of India in 1861. It was this distinction which led to the renaming of the Thomson Bridge to the Elgin Bridge, a name which it bears to this day. The first Elgin Bridge was demolished and replaced by a much wider construction to allow for heavier traffic in the 1920s. Elgin died in India in 1863.

Fowlie Road was named after Dr P Fowlie who, with such a name, was likely to be a Scot from Aberdeenshire.

In addition to a luxury hotel bearing his name, Sir Robert Fullerton, born in Edinburgh in 1773, lends his name to Fullerton Road and Fullerton Square.

George Street is named after the son-in-law of William Farquhar.

Gray Lane, Hamilton Road and Henderson Street are all associated with the Scottish firm Hamilton & Gray, George Henderson being one of the partners.

MacTaggart Road is named after W MacTaggart of Spottiswoode & Co, a Scottish trading company. He was one of the founders of the New Harbour Dock Company.

It is not clear, but Neil Road appears to be named after a 'hero' of the Indian Mutiny, Brigadier General James George Smith Neill. Born near Ayr in Scotland in 1810 and educated at the University of Glasgow, Neill, like many of his compatriots, enlisted in the service of the East India Company and had experience in the Burmese and Crimean Wars in 1852 and 1854. In 1857, the Indian Mutiny, or the First War of Indian Independence, broke out. He ruthlessly crushed the 'mutineers' in Benares and then moved on to Allahabad to relieve some trapped Europeans. At Cawnpore, Neill rigorously applied the death sentence on all prisoners with some brutality from whence he marched to Lucknow in intense heat and incessant rain. Neill courageously led from the front when his regiment was heavily engaged and, in the fury of the assault on entering the city, a bullet killed him. Courageous by any standard and heroic perhaps, depending on whose side you were on.

Outram Road is named in honour of Sir James Outram, the son of Benjamin Outram of Butterly, Derbyshire, England, who died in 1805 when his son James was only two years old. James's mother, daughter of Dr James Anderson, a noted Scottish writer on agriculture, returned to Scotland in 1810 and James was educated in Aberdeenshire at Udny school and Marischal College of Aberdeen. In 1819, he was offered a cadetship with a Indian regiment where he quickly gained experience of warfare and became known for his heroic actions which won him quick promotion. An imposing figure of six feet tall, he was known as 'highlander' by his fellow officers and it is no doubt that having been educated in north-east Scotland he would have picked up the native brogue and the words of the local Scots language known as the Doric. He was appointed Resident at Lucknow in 1854 and his name is connected strongly with the defence of Lucknow and the Indian War of Independence in 1857. In addition to his Scottish mother, education and upbringing, he also married a Scot – his cousin Margaret Clementina Anderson in India in 1835. In between his exploits in India he commanded troops in the Anglo-Persian War and a grateful nation rewarded him with a knighthood. He died on 11 March 1863 in Pau, France, and was buried in Westminster Abbey.

Purvis Street has connections with Jardine Matheson, the famous Scottish trading house which centred its business in Hong Kong and became a global player in business and commerce. John Purvis, born 1799, went to China with James Matheson but left him to form his own company, John Purvis and Co, in Singapore which, for many years, acted as Jardine Matheson's agents on the island. Purvis was active in the development of the new settlement having been appointed as a Magistrate by Raffles. He contributed to the foundation of the St Andrew's Church, pressed the government for land to build a Catholic church and was a founding subscriber, as many of the Scots traders were, of the library in 1844. His residence was in Kampong Glam along Beach Road, off which runs Purvis Street.

Read Bridge and Read Street are named after Scotsman William Henry Macleod Read. An exhaustingly active member of Singapore society, he was a special constable to deal with ethnic riots, a volunteer with the militia, appointed Dutch Consul, a member of the legislative counsel, a horse rider who won the inaugural race of the Singapore Turf Club, the organizer of the first rowing regatta, a Freemason, subscriber of the library, and a trustee of Raffles Institution. Read died in 1901. Perhaps he is the embodiment of the Scot that Scottish dramatist and playwright J M Barrie, the creator of *Peter Pan*, was thinking of in his play *What Every Woman Knows* when contemplating the difference between an Englishman and a Scotsman: 'You've forgotten the grandest moral attribute of a Scotsman, that he'll do nothing which might damage his career.' In the same play, speaking of a newly elected Member of Parliament, he added, 'My lady, there are few more impressive

sights in the world than a Scotsman on the make'.

In 1910, a plaque was placed in Read's memory in St Andrew's Cathedral for his outstanding contribution to Singapore.

Places in Scotland were also used to name houses, estates, districts and streets, no doubt chosen by expatriate Scots whose homesickness spurred them to select names that would remind them in a small way of cooler climes, different times and families and friends left behind.

Ballater Close. Ballater is a small town in north east Scotland not far from Aberdeen. The name has a Gaelic language derivation but the meaning is unclear. There are many place names beginning with bal, the word *baile* in Gaelic meaning town or village. Ballater, however, derives it name from the Gaelic *leiter* meaning hillside or long slope.

Balmoral Crescent, Park and Road are named after the Royal residence in Scotland. Purchased by Queen Victoria and her Consort Prince Albert it is owned personally by the monarch. Balmoral is a significant castle built in 1856 in the Scottish Baronial style.

Cluny Hill, Cluny and Cluny Road. In Gaelic, *cluain* is a meadow or pasture and the diminutive *cluaineag* is a lawn or patch of green. There are a number of Clunies in Scotland and Cluny is a further anglicised spelling of the word.

Dalvey Estate and Road, named after a residence owned by A L Johnston. *Dal* in Gaelic usually means field; the second part is not clear. Dalvey is also a place name in Perthshire

Dundee Road is named after the city on the east coast of Scotland; taking its name from the Gaelic *Dun Deagh*. *Dun* meaning fort and *deagh* is probably taken from a personal name deriving from the Gaelic word for fire. Famed for its links to India through its jute factories in the 19th century, Dundee now has a population of about 150,000 and boasts two universities and a renowned school of art.

Dunearn Close and Road. *Dun* means fort and *earn* could be either from the word *erin* meaning Ireland or from a pre-Celtic word associated with water which also provides the basis of the names Rhine and Rhone, two of the major rivers of Europe. Dunearn is also a place name from Fife in Scotland.

Kirk Terrace, demolished to build the School of the Arts in Bras Basah, was once near the Orchard Road Presbyterian Church. The Scottish church is known colloquially as the *kirk*, a word from old Norse *kirkja* meaning church. There are many towns in Scotland which have *kirk* as a prefix, with

William Henry Macleod Read. (Courtesy of the National Museum of Singapore, National Heritage Board)

Kirkton – meaning a number of houses around a church – being very common.

Melrose Drive is derived from a rural town in the Scottish Borders. It is famed for its ruined abbey, the resting place of the heart of King Robert the Bruce who brought independence to Scotland after his victory over the English at Bannockburn in 1314. Melrose is also the birthplace of seven-a-side rugby and is in the heart of Scott country as the celebrated novelist lived nearby. The name itself derives from the Gaelic *maol ros* meaning bare moor.

Strathmore appears in Singapore as Strathmore House in Tanglin Road and also in Strathmore Avenue. *Strath* means a broad valley and *mhor* is big, so Strathmore is a big, broad valley. It is also a Scottish place name covering a large swathe of fine farmland in Perth, Fife and Kinross.

Raeburn is another lowland name which was given by Charles Scott to his nutmeg plantation. Scott was a partner in the legal firm Napier & Scott. Raeburn Park could also be named after H H Raeburn of Guthrie & Co, the Scottish trading company. *Rae* is Scots for the roe deer and *burn* means a stream or small river. The name Raeburn appears frequently and is the name of a celebrated Scottish artist who was famed for his portraits of notable gentry and influential people in Scotland. Raeburn Place in Edinburgh is the site of the Edinburgh Academy, a well known school.

Still Road is a later addition to the roads named after Scotsmen. Alexander William Still took over editorship of *The Straits Times* in 1908, a post he held for 18 years. Still came from Aberdeen where he had started his career in journalism. His outspokenness was much admired and he was involved in a number of libel cases in defending what he regarded as the public interest. He retired in 1926 at the age of 66.

Many roads have, of course, been erased by the passage of time and progress. So, there are those bearing Scottish names which are on the record but no longer exist. Included among these are Farquhar Street after the first Resident of Singapore, Major General William Farquhar. This street in Kampong Glam was demolished in 1994 as the city developed. It is sad to see that one of the men responsible for the early development of Singapore is not remembered in any way or form. The self promotion of Raffles, and that of his widow after his demise, have conspired to deprive Farquhar of rightful recognition.

Fraser Street and Kerr Street, named after merchants from Scotland have gone the same way as Farquhar Street. Forfar Street and Clyde Street, likewise, have disappeared. Both are place names, Forfar being a small market and farming town in the county of Angus in east central Scotland and Clyde is the major river on which the city of Glasgow made its reputation in ship-building and engineering.

There is an area nestling between the Siglap Park connector, East Coast Road and Siglap Road, which recollects a small piece of the borders of Scotland. No less than a baker's dozen of streets in the Frankel Estate bear the names Wilton, Coldstream, Dunbar, Roseburn, Cheviot, Ettrick, Yarrow, Jedburgh, Dryburgh, Bowmont, Burnfoot, Lothian and Greenfield.

Wilton, where part of the author's own family hails from, used to be a separate burgh on the north side of the River Teviot beside Hawick but has now been subsumed into the larger parish. Burnfoot, likewise, has been subsumed into the town of Hawick which is one of the larger settlements in the Borders and, like all Border towns, is famed for its interest in rugby union. Clashes between rival Borders towns are always full of vigour and passion. The word *burn* in Scots means a small river.

Coldstream lies just on the north bank of the River Tweed which forms the border with England at this point. The meaning of the name is deceptively self evident, based on the famous salmon river on whose banks the town stands. However, the name appears to derive from its gaelic name of *An Sruthan Fuar* or in Scots, *Caustrim*. Being one of the nearest towns to England, in early days it was almost as popular as Gretna Green for runaway couples to get married as the law in Scotland is less demanding than in England. Coldstream is home to the Coldstream Guards, formed in 1650 by General George Monck, which has the distinction of being the oldest regiment in continuous service in the regular army.

Dunbar is on the east coast of Scotland and the name probably means fort on the height. *Dun* is Gaelic for fort and appears in many place names in Scotland. Occupying a strategic point on the sea routes to the east coast cities of Edinburgh (*Dun Edin* in Gaelic) and Dundee, Dunbar and its castle, dating from the 14th century, played a part in many wars and skirmishes between Scotland and its aggressive neighbour to the south. It is now a coastal holiday resort known for its bracing (i.e. freezing cold) air, and a number of fine golf courses.

Now just a ruin with little evidence remaining of its illustrious past, the castle was burned in 1214 and was heroically defended against the English by the Countess of Dunbar, known as Black Agnes, in 1338. Mary Queen of Scots came to the castle in the 1560s and it was ordered to be demolished in 1567 by an Act of Parliament.

Roseburn, Lothian and Greenfield are not in the same category as the others, not being specific places. Lothian possibly takes its name from the

legendary King Loth who controlled Lothian which covers an area from Edinburgh down to and possibly including the Borders. Roseburn is a place name from Perthshire but is also a district of Edinburgh on the western approach to the city on the banks of the river, Water of Leith. Nowadays, it is a quiet residential area close to the Murrayfield national rugby stadium where many fans before and after matches will descend on the famed Roseburn Bar to celebrate or, more likely, drown their sorrows. Greenfield is a pleasant name and there are some local namesakes in Scotland but none of any historical significance.

Cheviot Hill in Siglap takes its name from the Cheviot Hills which form the backbone of the Scottish Borders. They are wide, rolling hills of no great height but their impressively wide valleys with rivers and lochs, and smooth rounded tops are of great scenic beauty. Here were the extensive sheep farms on which the traditional woollen industry was based. Sir Walter Scott, who would be very familiar with this rolling landscape, described them in his novel *Rob Roy*: 'The Cheviots rose before me in frowning majesty; not in-

A drawing with the Cheviot Hills in the distance.

deed, with the sublime variety of rock and cliff which characterises mountains of the primary class, but huge, round-headed, and clothed with a dark robe of russet, gaining, by their extent and desolate appearance, an influence upon the imagination, as a desert district possessing a character of its own.' The hills extend down into the spine of England linking eventually with the central Pennine range.

Ettrick and Yarrow are two rivers in the Borders. Ettrick Water, boasting fine salmon and trout fishing, flows through the parish and village of Ettrick which is close to the birthplace of James Hogg the writer, known as the Ettrick Shepherd, his seminal work being *Private Memoirs and Confessions of a Justified Sinner* published in 1824. The Yarrow Water is a tributary of the Ettrick which is in turn a tributary of the major River Tweed. The Yarrow Valley was the birthplace of Mungo Park and Sir Walter Scott's residence Abbotsford is close by. No meaning is known for Ettrick but Yarrow is derived from continental Gaelic *gara* meaning rough or turbulent and gives its name also to the River Garonne in France.

Jedburgh and Dryburgh are two Borders market towns and both are blessed with magnificent abbeys, sadly in ruins. Jedburgh, now a town of about 4,000 people, was once a centre of pilgrimage associated with the abbey which was founded in 1147. It was sacked by English troops in the 16th century. Dryburgh Abbey was founded in 1150, was burned down by English troops in 1322, restored in 1385 and destroyed finally by the English in 1544. In spite of them being ruins, both abbeys are places of great beauty and tranquillity and draw many visitors every year. Sir Walter Scott, whose cousin gave his name to Scotts Road in Singapore, is buried in Dryburgh Abbey, as is Earl Douglas Haig whose name is remembered in Haig Road, Singapore.

Bowmont River rises in Scotland in the Cheviot Hills and flows through Yetholm across the English border and into the River Glen and thus, the North Sea.

FOUR

Colonial Gentlemen

We have looked in some detail at the early Residents, Farquhar and Crawfurd, but what of the other administrators of Scottish origin?

India was of huge importance to the Empire; known as the Jewel in the Crown, it dominated British Imperial history and ambition. And yet, less than a century after the legal union with England, the first three Governor-Generals of India were Scots and out of twelve Viceroys, seven were Scottish with many other Scots serving in junior positions. This pattern was echoed in the East Indies where those in positions of importance were predominantly Scottish. Of the first eight Resident Councillors of Singapore, covering the most influential and crucial years of the settlement's existence, five were Scottish.

By 1792, Scots made up one in nine of the East India Company civil servants, one in eleven soldiers and one in three officers. Generally throughout the British Empire the influence of Scots was of similar proportions. Nineteen of the 56 signatories of the American Declaration of Independence were Scots, and 75 percent of United States Presidents, including Barack Obama through a confirmed 17th century maternal ancestor, can claim some Scottish blood.

In addition to William Farquhar and Dr John Crawfurd, of the six Resident Councillors of the East India Company, three others were Scottish: Kenneth Murchison, Henry Somerset Mackenzie and Colonel Ronald MacPherson. Of the Straits Settlements, when under control of British India, two were Scottish: Robert Fullerton and Kenneth Murchison.

Sir Robert Fullerton, born in Edinburgh in 1773, was appointed the first Governor of the Straits Settlements in 1826 when Penang, Singapore and Malacca were grouped together to form the Straits Settlements. During his tenure from 1826 to 1830, he focused on raising revenue to make the Straits Settlements more self-sufficient and less reliant on the Indian Government. He devised methods such as new taxes on land as well as new fines and fees

Fullerton Building when it was the General Post Office, 1945. (Australian War Memorial) Overleaf: Tan Kim Seng Fountain in Fullerton Square, c 1889.

in the Law Courts. As expected, these were not popular moves. In 1829, the Straits merchants, keen to preserve Singapore's free port status, defeated Fullerton's proposals to impose export duties and stamp dues.

On the larger strategic front, he also ran up against the East India Company's policy of non-intervention in the Malay States, when he sought to check Siamese aggression in the Northern Malay States to protect British trade. Going against the Supreme Government's orders, Fullerton threatened Siam with war several times. His bold moves earned him a censure from the Supreme Government. Fullerton returned to Europe in 1830 and died in London a year later.

A fort built in 1829 at the mouth of the Singapore River was named after him. Fort Fullerton, designed to defend the settlement against naval attacks, was extended in 1843 after a sandstone monolith, the Singapore Stone, with an inscription possibly dating back to the 13th century was demolished. A fragment of this monolith is preserved in the National Museum of Singapore. The fort was demolished in 1873, and in 1928, a Victorian-style structure, called the Fullerton Building housing a range of tenants including the General Post Office, was built on the site.

Today, the grand luxury hotel The Fullerton Hotel, converted from Fullerton Building, sits on the land where Fort Fullerton once stood.

As for Kenneth Murchison, not much is recorded of his contributions as Resident Councillor of Singapore from 1833 to 1836, beyond presiding over the court system as a recorder (or a judge in those days) in the absence of an appointed professional judge. During his tenure, he was said to have spent much of his tenure away on holiday in South Africa, leaving his deputy and eventual successor Samuel Bonham to run the Straits Settlement.

Men of the Cloth

Scottish missionaries are often noted for their contributions to pioneering schools and planting churches across the British Empire, including in Singapore. Several important schools, such as the well-regarded Raffles Institution, and churches, such as the Orchard Road Presbyterian Church, were set up or influenced by Scottish missionaries. Their work was part of a wider movement that can be traced to the legacy of the Scottish Reformation.

The Scottish Reformation started in 1559 when John Knox returned from Geneva following his studies with John Calvin and Martin Luther. Harry Reid in his book *Reformation, The Dangerous Birth of the Modern World* informs us that Knox's work in Scotland brought a social and political revolution as well as a religious one. He adds that the

Scottish reformers had a 'visionary determination to place education at the very heart of their revolution. This education was to be democratic'. The Catholic monarchy in Scotland was weak and the true leader in the country became Knox. According to Reid, he was everything a leader should be – inspirational, charismatic, energetic and above all, visionary.

The Reformation resulted in the acceptance that Scotland was effectively a protestant state and the reforming zeal led to production of *The First Book of Discipline* which laid the groundwork for the democratic approach for which Knox strived. In this *First Book*, 'education was dealt with at length and with special enthusiasm' and what is more, medicine was added to the curriculum of Scotland's three universities of that time. 'Learning, knowledge and wisdom were to be, in theory at least, available to all'.

The church was a powerful force under Knox's charismatic leadership and although the *First Book* was not adopted by Parliament officially, it became generally accepted by the population as the church vigorously pushed and implemented its major tenets. It was radical and even utopian in its ambition; there was to be a concentration 'on self-restraint, self improvement, education, democracy and social inclusion' and, in time, these powerful emphases would produce a 'driven aspirational mentality in young Scots'.

The dark side was the influence of the church in creating, as some claimed, a dour hypocrisy, subservience and a control of private lives through parish churches, which all were required to attend, meting out discipline for often trivial offences. People still argue today about the baleful influence of Knox and Calvin on the psyche of Scottish people.

The overwhelming benefit of the Scottish Reformation, however, was that education became available to all and the levels of literacy were high in comparison with most other countries at the time. Each parishioner was spiritually independent and encouraged to be sceptical, have egalitarian values and be open minded.

Knox's view was that you cannot have a true democracy unless the people understand the issues. Not an uncommon view even today. Knox's work was so successful that Lord Macauley, the renowned British historian, in his celebrated *History of England*, points out: 'It began to be evident that the common people of Scotland were superior in intelligence to the common people of any country in Europe'. It was this literacy and 'intelligence' that contributed to Scots being in demand for important positions in Europe and wider afield.

The beginnings of the Protestant movement in Singapore could be traced to two Scotsmen, Reverend Dr William Milne and Dr Robert Morrison, who

1. Chinese Printing Office   2. English Printing Office   3. Chinese School   4. Western Gate of

were advancing the work of the London Missionary Society in the Far East. They first chose Malacca as a base in 1815, but moved it to Singapore in 1819.

Part of the mission's strategy was to set up schools and printing presses. In Malacca, Morrison and Milne established a school named the Anglo-Chinese College in 1818. The chief aim of the institution was the cultivation of Chinese and English literature, and the diffusion of Christianity.

Both Milne and Morrison applied themselves to learning Chinese. Milne, born in Aberdeenshire in 1785, once said: 'Learning the Chinese language requires bodies of iron, lungs of brass, heads of oak, hands of spring steel, eyes of eagles, hearts of apostles, memories of angels, and lives of Methuselah.' He persevered and soon produced the second complete Chinese version of the Bible together with Morrison, the first Christian Protestant missionary in China. He subsequently also produced many Chinese tracts. Milne also learnt Malay, chiefly from Munshi Abdullah who described Milne as having the deportment of a gentleman, his conversation polite and refined. A pioneer in Chinese translation, Dr Morrison is renowned for his translation of the Bible into Chinese and his compilation of a Chinese dictionary.

In spite of his initial rejection by the East India Company, they did eventually provide considerable financial support for his work by paying him a stipend and giving support for his dictionary.

So impressed was Raffles with their work at the Anglo-Chinese College that in 1823, he discussed with Morrison his desire to move it to Singapore. Unfortunately for Raffles, this plan failed to materialise because of his illness that year and his unexpectedly quick return to England. However, his dream was kept alive with the founding of the Raffles Institution, which was modeled on the Anglo-Chinese College in Malacca.

Morrison is credited with the co-founding with Raffles in 1823 of the Raffles Institution, the earliest centre of pre-tertiary learning in Singapore. Whilst their intention and legacy was a benevolent one, Mrs Morrison records in her *Memoirs of the Life and Labours of Robert Morrison* the typically colonial, condescending impetus for the initiative, and said of the discussion between Raffles and Morrison, 'On many subjects their views coincided, and for the moral condition of their fellow-creature in these benighted regions, both were alike solicitous'. She added, 'The result of their conference was, the formation of an Institution similar to the one established at Malacca'. This was the one established by Dr Milne.

The Reverend Hutchings of Penang was also present at the discussion and in respect of the newly conceived Institution he said: 'It may, in the

Top left: Anglo Chinese College, Malacca. Bottom left: William Milne.

hand of Providence, be one of the instruments by which he will accomplish the prediction, "that the knowledge of the Lord shall cover the earth as the waters cover the sea."

Mrs Morrison further recorded a series of remarks made by Dr Morrison, including the more philosophical point that, 'Some men will not plant a tree because it cannot attain its proper size in their lifetime; but the tree of knowledge which we would plant, is not for our individual use alone, it is for the healing of those around us. Knowledge is not virtue; but knowledge is power, and should always be possessed by the virtuous to enable them to do good to others'.

The mission schools in Singapore had a strong welfare impetus, providing for those who could not afford proper schooling. They were responsible for the initial spread of English literacy among the local population, and might have made some small contribution to the high regard that mission schools is still held. The willingness of Scottish traders to pay for the schools is also a point to be noted. The first subscription to Raffles Institution included a number of them.

Scottish clergymen were strongly associated with education in Scotland; it was one of the main features of the Scottish Reformation that linked parish schools and the church and the striving for literacy. Drs Morrison and Milne have many parallels of Scottish ministers being involved in the founding of educational institutions; none perhaps more so than the Reverend John Witherspoon, born in the parish of Yester near Edinburgh in 1722 and a graduate of Edinburgh University. His reputation was such that in 1768 he was invited to become President of the College of New Jersey, now known as Princeton, a position which he held for 25 years until his death. He is regarded as one of the founders of the United States of America being one of the signatories to the Declaration of Independence.

Other Scottish presbyterian missions, notably in the African continent, included that of the renowned David Livingston, born in Blantyre, and Mary Slessor, a mill girl from Dundee. The educational work which accompanied these missionaries was what led to the widely held belief at the time that Scottish education was the best in the world.

There was a succession of Scottish ministers at the Presbyterian Church in Singapore, one of the more notable being the Reverend George Murray Reith who served as minister in Singapore from 1889 to 1896. Born in 1863 in Aberdeen, he was educated at Aberdeen and Edinburgh Universities, and is best remembered for producing the first guide book to Singapore, the *Handbook to Singapore*, first published in 1892.

Dr Robert Morrison.

Reith's relatively long tenure of seven years is regarded as unusual, so he must have been particularly popular. As well as teaching at the church, he spoke at the Boustead Institute and gave lectures on history, Scotland and on Biblical criticism. He was also vocal on matters of principle such as Sunday working and gambling.

He continued to write for the Singapore newspapers after his return to Scotland in 1898, where he had been appointed as minister to St Cuthbert's United Free Church in Edinburgh and was active in church matters until his death in 1948. He was a keen walker and wrote a guidebook to the walks in the Pentland Hills to the south-west of Edinburgh entitled *The Breezy Pentlands*.

R L Stevenson wrote often about the Pentland Hills, close as they are to the city of his birth. Stevenson, like so many of his countrymen, endured a self-imposed exile in the South Seas but again, like so many of his compatriots, could not forget his homeland. Stevenson rather pointedly commented on emigration as being 'nothing more agreeable to picture and nothing more pathetic to behold'. Reith was obviously an active and keen walker, witness his guidebook of the Pentlands, and no doubt in the heat and humidity of Singapore his mind would stray to the cool breeze of the hills of home.

Stevenson captures the feeling of nostalgia and homesickness beautifully in his letter to fellow Scot and writer J M Barrie, 'It is a singular thing that I should live here in the South Seas under conditions so new and so striking, and yet my imagination so continually inhabits the cold old huddle of grey hills from which we come...'

Another early missionary to Singapore was the Reverend G H Thomson whose nationality is not determined but Thomson is a predominantly Scottish name. He also was involved in the establishment of the Raffles Institution and was one of the first subscribers. In addition, he and his wife set up one of the first schools in Singapore in a very informal manner. In two rooms in their house, near the corner of Bras Basah and North Bridge Roads, the Reverend Thomson had a class of six boys and Mrs Thomson taught a class of six girls on the upper floor.

The publication *100 Years of Singapore* provides some informative detail on the denominations of the churches and congregations and the importance placed by the merchants, not only in having worthy places of worship but of having the right denomination.

Europe, for centuries, had been riven by wars to establish and defend rights of worship and the colonists, keenly aware of this history and however liberal they might have been, would have been more comfortable with the

Protestantism which came with the Scottish Reformation and was protected vigorously in the Act of Union by the Church of Scotland. Catholicism had not been eradicated by the Reformation but it was decidedly a minority.

The following extract from *100 Years of Singapore* informs us that 'in the early years of the colony, Presbyterians, who have always formed an important section of the European community, worshipped with Episcopalians in the mission chapel of the London Missionary Society at the corner of Bras Basah Road and North Bridge Road. The services were conducted by the resident missionaries, by visiting clergymen, and later by the Government Chaplain. In 1834, when it was proposed to erect an Episcopal Church worthy of the Colony, and for which the Government had provided a site, Presbyterians gave substantial support for the scheme.

'In November 1846 the Scotsmen of the Colony, among whom were representatives of the three leading denominations of the homeland Established Church, Free Church and United Presbyterian Church at a numerous and harmonious meeting resolved to get a minister for European work from any of the Scottish churches. The meeting also passed a resolution assuring the chaplain, Rev Mr Moule, that the step they were taking was not to be interpreted as dissatisfaction with him, but as preference for their own denomination. The inference is that Presbyterians were accustomed at that time to attend worship in St Andrew's Church. The newspapers gave friendly support to the scheme, assuring Presbyterians that members of the Church of England would show towards them the same liberality as they had shown when St Andrew's Church was being built.'

The final comment refers to the generosity of Scots in contributing significantly to the cost of the church and its subsequent naming after Scotland's Patron Saint in recognition.

The Orchard Road Presbyterian Church, nick-named the "Scots Church", is the earliest Presbyterian church in Singapore. The congregation started with a sizeable proportion of Scots, mainly sailors and soldiers. The first service was conducted in 1856 by Reverend Thomas McKenzie Fraser at the London Missionary Society's chapel on Bras Basah Road. The church moved to its current location on Orchard Road when the building was erected in 1878.

The scholar John Leyden is referred to in relation to his friendship with Raffles and his wife. As well as being a trained doctor, botanist and linguist of exceptional ability he was also a deeply devout man and, recognising his extraordinary linguistic abilities, was engaged by the British and Foreign Bi-

Overleaf: *Handbook to Singapore* (1892) by George Murray Reith with its map insert, and a postcard of Stamford Road showing the Methodist Publishing House, c 1910.

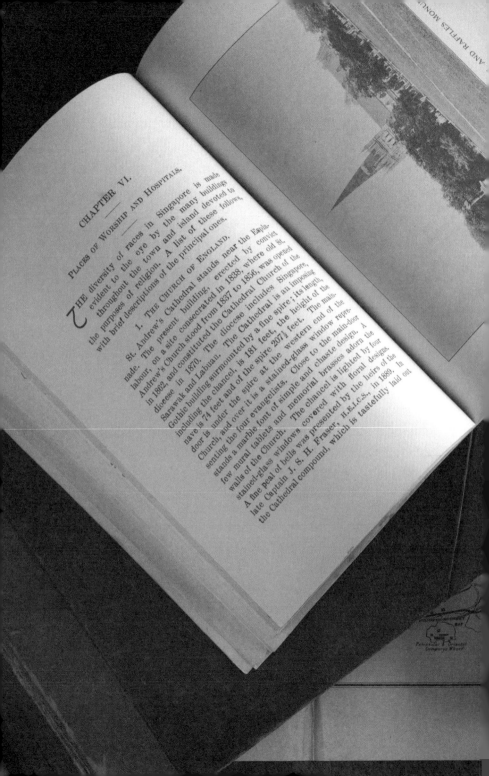

CHAPTER VI.

PLACES OF WORSHIP AND HOSPITALS.

THE diversity of races in Singapore is made evident to the eye by the many buildings throughout the town and island devoted to the purposes of religion. A list of these follows, with brief descriptions of the principal ones.

1. THE CHURCH OF ENGLAND. — St. Andrew's Cathedral stands near the Esplanade. The present building, erected by convict labour, on a site consecrated in 1838, where old St. Andrew's Church stood from 1837 to 1856, was opened in 1862, and constituted the Cathedral Church of the diocese in 1870. The diocese includes Singapore, Sarawak and Labuan. The Cathedral is an imposing Gothic building surmounted by a fine spire ; its length, including the chancel, is 181 feet, the height of the nave is 74 feet and of the spire 207½ feet. The main-door is under the spire at the western end of the Church, and over it is a stained-glass window representing the four evangelists. Close to the main-door stands a marble font of simple and chaste design. A few mural tablets and memorial brasses adorn the walls of the Church. The chancel is lighted by four stained-glass windows covered with floral designs. A fine peal of bells was presented by the heirs of the late Captain J. S. H. Fraser, H.E.I.C.S., in 1889. In the Cathedral compound, which is tastefully laid out

ble Society to translate certain books of the New Testament into Siamese, Macasser, Bugis, Afghan, Rakheng, Maldivian and Jeghatai. In little more than a year, he was able to deliver all four Gospels into Maldivian, Matthew and Mark into Pushtu and Mark into Baloch, Macasser and Bugis; sadly his untimely death in Java in 1811 cut short his work in this task.

The Professionals

Scottish teachers, engineers, doctors and lawyers found positions of influence across the Empire. Professor T Devine in his work on the Scottish diaspora points out that even as late as the 1920s, Scotland educated three times as many university graduates as England and at that time had six universities compared to England's two. Scotland's education system was more broadly based, meritocratic and practical, rewarded talent and produced many more graduates than could be absorbed within the country.

In Singapore, we see the impact of Scottish professionals in the early days and their legacy down to the present time. Their investment in businesses in America, South Africa, Canada, Australia and New Zealand had familiarised Scottish business people with the systems, instruments and policies of doing business overseas. Entrepreneurs overseas need only contact a Scottish lawyer who brought to bear not only his legal skills but, in his wake, an entire syndicate of people willing to invest in new ventures. They were comfortable with the risks and, in many instances, were dealing with their fellow countrymen regardless of how far from home they might have been. All of this oiled the wheels of finance, the prerequisite to trade.

James Guthrie Davidson was born in 1838 in Menmuir, Forfar. He was the nephew of merchant James Guthrie who, with his eldest cousin, ran Guthrie & Co, Asia's oldest mercantile firm. J G Davidson read Law at the University of Edinburgh and, in February 1861, became an advocate (the Scottish equivalent of barrister at law) and member of the Solicitors to the Supreme Court, a Scottish membership body for lawyers pleading at court.

Presumably influenced by his uncle's trading activities in the East, he quickly decided to emulate his success and set sail for Singapore, arriving in late June 1861. Clearly a young man in a hurry, he was called to the bar of the Straits Settlements on first July of the same year and 27 days later was in partnership with Robert Carr Woods, at least 20 years his senior and the first editor of *The Straits Times*, doing business as Woods & Davidson, Singapore's first law firm.

In his haste to depart Scottish shores, the no doubt normally assiduous Mr Davidson, omitted to inform the Society of Solicitors to the Supreme

Court that he would no longer require membership. His subscriptions remained unpaid and he was struck off the Society's rolls on 17 October 1879 when he was recorded as being 'dead or at least subsidy in arrears for many years'. On informing the current librarian of the Society of Solicitors, the author was thanked for allowing them to amend their records as Davidson's emigration to Singapore was the likely reason he stopped paying his dues.

In 1877, following the demise of Woods, another partner, Bernard Rodyk, was engaged and thus the firm became Rodyk & Davidson as it remains to this day, one of the largest and most prestigious legal firms in the city.

Davidson died in a tragic accident at the relatively young age of 53 years after being thrown from his buggy in Orchard Road on his way to church. Ardmore Park is named after his residence which he had called Ardmore. The word is an anglicisation of the Gaelic *Aird Mhor* where *aird* means a high place or promontory and *mhor*, big or great. Davidson was also the first Resident of Selangor in the Federated Malay States from 1875 to 1878. Davidson Road in Singapore is named after him.

Other Scottish lawyers who made their name in Singapore include Alexander Muirhead Aitken, son of a farmer from Torphichen, near Linlithgow who, like Davidson, was a graduate of the University of Edinburgh. Although the firm no longer bore his name from the date of his retirement in 1879, he was a founder of the partnership Donaldson & Birkinshaw which continues to practise successfully in Singapore to this day.

Abraham Logan, born in Berrywell or Hatton Hall, Berwickshire in 1816, was another lawyer from Scotland who served Singapore with distinction. He was involved in advising the British Government on matters such as constitutional and judicial reform in the Straits Settlements on its transfer to the Colonial Office and on economic points relating to taxation and currency. He was also secretary to the Singapore Chamber of Commerce for 18 years from its founding in 1850. Not content with all, that he was also the editor of the *Singapore Free Press* from 1843 until 1865 where he was highly regarded for his integrity and high journalistic standards and championing issues with the authorities of the day.

Together with his brother, James Richardson Logan, he was one of the first subscribers to the Singapore Library in 1844. Buckley recorded in August of 1843: 'It was proposed to start a public library by subscription'. The following August a public meeting was held and it was agreed that the library would be housed in the Singapore Institution. Of the total of 32 first shareholders, 18 were Scots.

The creation of a public library foreshadows Andrew Carnegie's founding, about 40 years later, of a gift to create a library in his home town of Dunfermline, Scotland, and thereafter more than 2,500 libraries throughout the world. Carnegie's unprecedented wealth, made principally in American steel, was followed by equally unprecedented philanthropy. Carnegie is credited with the adage that, 'if a man dies wealthy, he dies disgraced'. Logan's aim, in common with Carnegie's, was to promote the principle of self help and provide the means for people who wish to help themselves to achieve their goals.

Carnegie believed that progress lay in individuals meeting their moral obligations to themselves and to society; he held strong views on inherited wealth, believing that the sons of prosperous businessmen were rarely as talented as their fathers and that leaving money to their children was a waste of a resource which could be used to benefit society.

These were not new principles dreamed up by Carnegie although he was by far the most assiduous in applying them; they are however, characteristic of the thinking of Scotland and its people, through its legal and educational systems and its distinctively democratic church, all of which had survived the union with England.

Singapore's first lawyer was William Napier (no relation to Walter John Napier of Drew & Napier), appointed in 1833. A Scot from Edinburgh, he arrived in Singapore in 1831 and was one of the founders of the *Singapore Free Press* and a shareholder of the Raffles Library.

William Napier.

Napier Road, which originally led to his house, is named after him.

His father McVey Napier, a lawyer and legal scholar, was also an editor of the *Encyclopaedia Britannica*, first published in Edinburgh in 1771. Among Mcvey's seven sons, two travelled to Singapore. The elder, David Skene Napier, arrived in the early 1820s and was appointed magistrate by Raffles in 1823.

The Medical Fraternity
Scotland was renowned for its medical schools which trained many more students than could be employed locally as well as training doctors from overseas. Scottish medicine and methods had a similar influence in the Empire to those of education and the church. It must have been quite a shock to the system for doctors, trained in the hallowed confines of the cold, grey dampness of Edinburgh, to burst forth into the Empire, replete with pride and confidence, with their newly achieved scroll tucked safely in their bags, into the heat and dust of India or the humid, sultry and downright wet heat of Singapore.

Doctors in a Scottish town or village, who were regarded as pillars of the community, along with the dominie (schoolmaster), and the minister (pastor), would be one of the few to whom people would turn for advice, guidance and information. Their introduction to Singapore, after a harrowing sea journey of many months – if they survived it – must have been a baptism of fire as they were rapidly introduced to a bewildering array of deadly infections and endemic tropical diseases.

A number of Scottish-trained doctors were brave enough to head to Singapore. One of the earliest was Dr J William Montgomerie, born 1797 in Irvine, Ayrshire, the home county of the celebrated national poet of Scotland, Robert Burns. Montgomerie graduated from the University of Edinburgh in 1817 and left for Calcutta and the Bengal Infantry as a surgeon the following year. His interests took him almost immediately to Singapore where he arrived in 1819. Montgomerie became a prominent citizen of the new settlement, becoming involved in the community, schools, church, St Andrew's Day obervance and sports activity. A keen sailor, he became the inaugural president of the Singapore Yacht Club in 1826.

As well as being a surgeon of some note, like most early settlers, he had more than one string to his bow; he was an entrepreneur and owned significant land for nutmeg plantations in what is now the Duxton Hill area of Singapore. Duxton was the name of one of his houses on the plantation as was Craig. His house was built by Hugh Syme or Ferguson. The plantation was sold up and divided after his death. Dr Montgomerie, who provided samples of nutmeg, mace and other spices together with a treatise on their cultivation, was presented with a Gold Medal by the Royal Society of Arts in London for his information and advice.

Dr Montgomerie was the first European to notice the properties of gutta percha and took some plants back to Europe for further investigation. The plasticity of the product derived from the plant allows cables to be coated as well as making of moulds. The most important application at the time was its use in the insulation of telegraphic cables but the most interesting to a Scot would have been the quality which allowed it to be used in the manufacture of golf balls. The first use of gutta percha in a golf ball was by J Patterson in Scotland in 1845. The new style of ball, replacing balls stuffed with feathers, was called a 'gutty', and was in use until about 1900 when the 'gutty' itself was replaced by new production technology.

Dr Montgomerie's home was on the side of the present Padang and Esplanade area where other senior officials, such as the first Resident Farquhar, made their residence. Montgomerie stayed in Singapore from 1819 to 1843 and thereafter practised as a surgeon in Burma, China and India. He died of cholera in 1856 and is buried in Calcutta.

Dr Robert Little, whose father was an Edinburgh lawyer, was the eldest of three brothers who settled in Singapore and devoted most of his life to the new settlement before retiring in London where he died in 1888. In common with other settlers, his interests were wide and he undertook research, not only into the causes of some of the tropical diseases affecting the population, but also in horticulture, particularly scrutinising the diseases of the nutmeg tree which had caused some devastation to the previously reliable crops.

He had an ambition to found a sanitorium on Gunung Pulai in Johore but support for this was not forthcoming. It was during a foray into the interior to survey the feasibility of such a venture that the party, which included John Turnbull Thomson, came across a large ferocious beast which could not at first be seen clearly because of the dense forest. After several futile attempts to sight the beast and bring him down, the animal was trapped up against some trees and shot by one of the convicts accompanying the party. It was a rhinoceros.

Dr Little purchased a house on Institution Hill on River Valley Road where he lived for about 35 years; he called his residence Bonnygrass, a good Scottish name no doubt to remind him of home. His partner Dr Martin, lived in Annanbank, also on River Valley Road, named rather wistfully after the fine river in south-west Scotland which flows through Moffat and into

The Dispensary founded by Thomas Robertson and Lim Boon Keng. (Archive Collection/Jan Eaton) Top left: Dr Robert Little. Top right: Dr William Montgomerie. Bottom: David Galloway.

THE DISPENSARY

Singapore 190

the Solway not far from the county town of Dumfries.

Doctors, as they did back home, played a vital part in the life of the community. In Buckley's *Anecdotal History of Old Times in Singapore*, we read time and time again of the involvement of Dr Little in decisions involving everything from pirates, siting of bridges, schools and even comments on climate, specifically the relative levels of rainfall in different years and parts of the year. The Little brothers were also involved in trading and collectively established the store still operating under the name of John Little in Singapore to this day.

In 1859, Dr Little was joined in partnership by Dr John Hutchinson Robertson of Edinburgh. Dr Robertson was later succeeded by his son Dr Thomas Murray Robertson who was born in Singapore but sent to Edinburgh for his education at George Watson's College and thereafter the University of Edinburgh Medical School where he qualified MB and CM in 1883 and as MD in 1887.

Thomas Murray Robertson formed a partnership with Lim Boon Keng, another noted physician and graduate of Edinburgh University Medical School, at The Dispensary in Raffles Place founded by the elder Robertson in 1879 which quickly became one of the most respected practices in Singapore. The practice remained in operation until well into the 1900s. Thomas Murray Robertson, in addition to his duties as a physician, was appointed Coroner and Police Surgeon and lectured at the King Edward VII College of Medicine which was established in 1905 in Singapore.

Robertson Quay, a significant area of warehouses along the Singapore River, now a lively entertainment hub buzzing with nightclubs, bars and restaurants, is named in memory of Dr Thomas Murray Robertson.

The celebrated Sir Arthur Conan Doyle, the creator of the fictional detective Sherlock Holmes, who relied on deductive reasoning to solve curious and esoteric mysteries was, in addition to being a successful author, a physician trained at the Edinburgh Medical School. The literary Holmes was modelled directly on one of the lecturers at the Edinburgh Medical School, namely Dr Joseph Bell JP, DL, FRCS, who very successfully practised a heightened form of observation and deduction in examining patients and their symptoms.

Conan Doyle worked briefly for Dr Bell in 1877, and Dr T M Robertson, and indeed probably Dr Lim Boon Keng, were likely to have been students at a similar time as Conan Doyle and therefore, also students of the celebrated Dr Bell and thereby influenced by his methods of logical deduction in examining patients. It is tempting to imagine this could have been a factor in Dr

Robertson's appointment as Coroner and Police Surgeon in Singapore and that he drew from those skills in not only conducting the gruesome business that no doubt came his way, but also imparted the same skills to his students in his lectures at the King Edward VII College of Medicine.

Edinburgh might well have been famed for its medical school and people of intellect in the 19th century. However, it was still a difficult place to live and doctors were probably relieved to find some tropical warmth as they populated various parts of the Empire.

Edinburgh's nickname has been for many years, Auld Reekie or Old Smokey in English. In 1819, contemporary with the first British settlement in Singapore, the poet Robert Southey joined the Scottish engineer Thomas Telford on a tour of Scotland. His journal records his view of Edinburgh, 'The view from this hotel in the morning when the fires are just kindled, is probably the finest smokescape that can anywhere be seen. Well may Edinburgh be called Auld Reekie! and the houses stand so one above another, that none of the smoke wastes itself upon the desert air before the inhabitants have derived all advantage of its odour and smuts. You might smoke bacon by hanging it out of the window.'

Dr David James Galloway, born in Scotland in 1858, took over from Dr T M Robertson in 1885. Dr Galloway was a gold medallist of the Medical School in Edinburgh where he was elected a fellow of the Royal College of Physicians, publishing treatises on various medical matters. Like the other doctors mentioned, his interests and activities stretched far beyond the bounds of the practice of general medicine. He was a member of the Legislative Council and his efforts in the ambulance service were rewarded by the St John Ambulance Association. In 1896, Galloway started his own clinic in Raffles Place which was named the British Dispensary. He was knighted in 1924 for his services.

Galloway was a confidante of Sultan Abu Bakar of Johore and he retired to Malaya but Dr Galloway died in Singapore at the age of 84 in 1943 when Singapore was under Japanese occupation.

While most of the Scottish professionals who came to Singapore were male, women were strongly represented in the healthcare sector. One Scotswoman who stands out for making a powerful contribution to improving healthcare in Singapore was Ida Mabel Murray Simmons.

Simmons, born in 1881, was Singapore's first Public Health Nurse and was credited for transforming maternal and infant health care standards in Singapore at a time when infant mortality was acutely high. Trained in Edinburgh's Royal Infirmary, she joined the Straits Settlements Medical Department in December 1926. When Simmons first arrived, she encountered a population with poor health and hygiene who were suspicious of Western medicine. Out of every 1,000 babies born in 1927, 263 babies died, with malnutrition of infants and mothers being a primary cause.

Simmons learned Malay and set out to educate families on infant health. On her first year, she managed to persuade the authorities to set up a mobile dispensary. It travelled with her to the rural villages as she made house calls. Simmons supervised the recruitment and training of many new nurses and midwives, especially Asians. Over time, she broke through the cultural barriers and sensitivities to Western medicine, improved health services in rural areas, and sharply brought down the infant mortality rate.

During the Japanese Occupation of Singapore from 1942-1945, Simmons was interned at Sime Road Camp, where she sewed 3,000 pairs of trousers for male prisoners. After the Occupation, she went back to rebuilding the infant health services which had suffered under the Japanese. Infant mortality had worsened but the damage was soon reversed under her care.

By the time she retired in 1948, she had established a network of 17 health centres operated by a team of local nurses. This became part of the Institute of Health in Outram Road in 1958. That very year, Simmons died in the town of Aberfoyle in Scotland.

DERRICK, G. A.,
Public Accountant,
Local Secretary—The Raub Australian Gold Mining Company, Limited;
Secretary—The Bersawah Gold Mining Company, Limited;
Secretary—The South Raub Gold Mining Syndicate, Limited;
Secretary—Sipiau Tin Co., Ltd.
A Liquidator of The Tanjong Pagar Land Company, Ltd., (in Liquidation)
A Liquidator of The Straits Insurance Company, Ltd., (in Liquidation)
Gresham House, Battery Road.
Hon. Agent—Shipmasters Society, London

G A Derrick and his entry in *Buku Merah*, Singapore's business gazette.

Accountants and Others

Scotland has a reputation for producing accountants of ability with a strong, practical and no-nonsense approach to business. As in other professions, accountants went out from Scotland across the globe to practice but, unusually, there seem to be very few who journeyed to Singapore. Scotland was an early starter in the profession of accountancy having formed the Institute of Chartered Accountants of Scotland in 1854, many years before any other nation. Membership of this prestigious body alone use the designatory letters CA for Chartered Accountant.

Alexander James Gunn was born in the Watten parish of Caithness in the remote northern part of Scotland between the small townships of Thurso and Wick, on 30 June 1840. His father was a minister of the Free Church and we know that A J Gunn was unsurprisingly, a staunch Presbyterian. For many years in Singapore, he was the Secretary of the Chamber of Commerce and was in business or associated with or employed Mr G A Derrick, who eventually formed his own firm which was an early precursor of the major accountancy practice of now Ernst & Young. There are notices in the newspapers indicating Gunn's activities as a Trustee in Bankruptcy and in other business matters but little evidence remains of his work. He retired in 1907 but returned to Singapore following the death of his wife and he himself died in Singapore on 28 November 1917.

One of the key tasks in a busy port must be the work of the pilot, understanding the tides, unusual weather conditions and shifting banks at or near entrances to the main port as they guided ships in and out of tricky waters. Described as the 'doyen of Singapore pilots' when he retired in 1929, Captain Alexander Snow was born in 17 James Square, Edinburgh, on 26 April 1861. His father was a master flesher (butcher), a trade which the young Alexander obviously didn't get involved in as he went to sea at the age of 16, serving an apprenticeship on a sailing vessel before heading out to the East. He became a marine pilot in Penang in 1891 where he stayed for two years before moving to Singapore. According to *Spaces of the Dead*, he died on 29 December 1937 and was buried in Singapore with a large crowd attending his funeral.

The Traders

Before the Victorian era, after which old barriers began to crumble just a little, anyone 'in trade' was considered to be beneath contempt. If you were in trade you had to work for a living, were not a 'gentleman' and hence worthy only of disdain and put into the same category as natives, dogs and servants. The high-minded clubs, which would almost certainly exclude women from membership, would also in the early days be closed to mere tradesmen. Many melodramas employed as their central theme the problems caused by associating, or not, with those from lower classes and the strict social divisions of the 'upstairs downstairs' mentality which still lingers to some extent today.

It is ironic then that traders and merchants were not only the ones that oiled the wheels of the British Empire but they were the ones who provided the engine and the fuel to run it. It was trade that drove the East India Company to establish strongholds in the East and force its way into China after its exploitation of India. If it was the protection from the might and skill of the Royal Navy that allowed trade to ply safely to and from far off shores, it was the merchants who were in the vanguard and who died in their droves in tropical lands.

It was for trade that Singapore had been founded. All of the early searching throughout the region, the work of hydrographers mapping sea routes, armies quelling natives and rebellions, navies providing protection, all initially supported the monopoly of the East India Company and to make money. However philanthropic some traders might have been once they became wealthy, it is likely that their primary aim was to make money.

Singapore was chosen for its strategic position on the trade routes from the East to Europe and its natural advantages of having a good harbour, safe anchorages and fresh water. The early traders were attracted here for these reasons and took full advantage of them.

In the essay, 'Sino-British Mercantile Relations in Singapore's Entrepôt Trade', from *Studies in the Social History of China and South East Asia: Essays in Memory of Victor Purcell*, Chiang Hai Ding points out that, 'The foreign trade of Singapore can be divided into two sections; the European or Western and the Asian or largely Chinese and partly Indian. The European merchants handled the imports from and exports to Western countries; their trade was conducted mainly at the wharves in the New Harbour and their shops were concentrated in Raffles Place.' The Chinese traders, by contrast, handled the distribution of materials from Singapore to the rest of Asia and the collection of their goods in Singapore. Their businesses were concentrated on the Singapore River around Boat Quay.

The Chinese, like the British, also had need of a port to handle their trade and were no doubt equally impressed by the natural features of Singapore and its geographical position. Some of them went into partnership with European companies, and from Europe the majority of the first companies were run by Scots who had already built up experience in Malaya, India and the Americas.

They had valuable experience of financing trade in different cultures and were knowledgeable of the varied business cycles of different commodities.

Scots would have been demanding to ensure that they got what they needed to do business. Cheong Suk-Wai is probably only slightly unfair when she says in the story of Rodyk's law firm, *Rodyk – 150 Years*, that the merchants in Singapore, 'mostly no-nonsense Scots – were first-class moaners who clamoured for better governance and security but refused to pay the taxes that would finance their demands.' Nothing much has changed in Singapore – business people will always seek benefits to enhance their profit generation, but the record of the Scots in supporting education, churches and libraries suggests that it was not all one way.

Philanthropy was embedded in the way of thinking of the early Scots traders who, in addition to supporting activities in Singapore, did not forget their homeland. On 16 July 1832, there was a great storm off the Shetland Isles which resulted in the loss of 17 boats and 105 crewmen. The news of this disaster would have taken many months to reach the Singapore Shetlanders but they responded as one might expect and made a collection. The donation was recorded in *The Shetland Times* of 1834: 'It is a fact illustrative of the strong feelings of interest and attachment entertained by British subjects in all parts of the world towards their native land, that the sum of 275 Spanish dollars have been subscribed and remitted to this country by the inhabitants of Singapore, in the Indian Ocean, for the relief of the widows and children of the unfortunate fishermen who perished upwards of a year since off the coast of Shetland.'

With sound management in the early days and the enterprise of mainly Scots traders, the port and all related business activity in Singapore thrived. The free port meant that duties and taxes were not levied and this attracted trade from surrounding areas. Penang declined and the Dutch found that their port at Rhio quickly withered in the shadow of Singapore as Chinese traders shifted their business to the new settlement. In the first two and a half years, *100 Years of Singapore* tells us that as many as '2889 vessels entered and cleared from the port'.

Junks from China sailed in on the North East Monsoon bringing tea, silk, and pottery wares; Chinese merchants managed this end of the trade and sent the junks back with goods from Britain and India mixed with exotic local produce. Aromas of cloves, rice, opium, pepper, cotton, foods and tin would combine with the sweat of coolies and deck hands as the heavy end of trade was performed with a view to profit for all involved. Barter, exchange

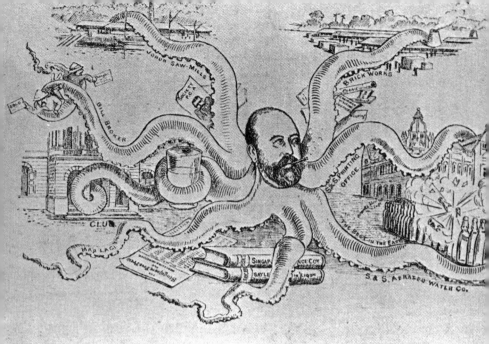

OUR JOLLY OLD OCTOPUS.

and a hundred watchful eyes on weighing and counting as bales, loads, carts and bundles were lifted, dragged, rolled, hoisted, heaved and carried from ship to sampan to godown and out again to waiting clippers, junks and East Indiamen.

A glance at the *Singapore Free Press and Mercantile Advertiser* of 16 March 1843 shows the range of produce on offer. For the mariners there were anchors, grapnels, canvas and steering compasses as well as nautical almanacs, lunar tables and charts, paints and cordage, twine and oils. Riders might be attracted by the 'large chestnut saddle horse, warranted quiet' or perhaps one of the 'three well-bred Sydney horses' or for the better heeled, one of the many gigs, gharries or carriages in which one might have sported the latest 'fashionable beaver hats and caps'. A colourful Japanese silk cloak as a gift for one's spouse and for the peckish there was 'Irish salt beef and pork' and to wash it all down you could select from hogsheads of beer, sherry, port, Madeira, claret or sauternes and finish off nicely with some brandy or gin, smoking a Manila Cheroot by candlelight whilst wearing an imported straw hat.

The Singapore Chamber of Commerce was formed in February 1837 to look after the commercial interests of traders. The founding Chairman of the Chamber was the Scot, Alexander Laurie Johnston, and his example was carried on by a number of eminent Scots in later years. The historian of the Chamber comments that, 'the expatriate business community was dominated by the Scottish'. The names of subsequent Chairmen include W H Read, Thomas Scott, Samuel Gilfillan, James Guthrie, Charles Spottiswoode and William Ramsay Paterson, all merchants from Scotland who spent a considerable period of their lives in Singapore.

One of Singapore's favourite thirst quenchers in present times is a cool and refreshing Tiger Beer brewed in 1931 by Malayan Breweries Ltd, a joint venture between Heineken International and Fraser & Neave. In mid-2012, a protracted and, belying the efficacy of the product, heated takeover battle between several major players involving the later incarnation of Malayan Breweries, Asia Pacific Breweries, the owners of the Tiger brand, was played out in the world markets. The parties battling it out for control of a stake of APB were players in a world market involving European brewers and one group led by a billionaire Thai businessman.

The relative humidity in Singapore rarely falls below 80 percent and, as a consequence, there are a lot of prodigiously thirsty people; the companies from Europe, no doubt aware of this, and wanting to take advantage, aimed to ensure that they had a good share of what, in spite of ubiquitous

Cartoon of John Fraser's business empire (National Archives of Singapore) and an advertisement for Fraser & Neave.

air-conditioning, continues to be a growing market. This lucrative market was spotted by two enterprising Scotsmen, Mr Fraser and Mr Neave, who not unaware that the thirst promoted by a warm and humid climate required to be assuaged, established a drink company, the eponymous Fraser & Neave Company.

John Fraser, a native of Wigtown in south-west Scotland joined a bank in the local market town of Newton Stewart. He became involved in a number of banking enterprises with David Chalmers Neave who was attracted to the relatively new British colony of Singapore. Alexander Laurie Johnston was also from this area of Scotland and had recently retired there and it is not unreasonable to imagine that a banker in Newton Stewart would have come across Mr Johnston and been inspired to travel to Singapore.

The first venture which Fraser & Neave founded in 1865 was a printing works and thereafter a number of other opportunities were taken up. In response to the diversity of interests and his good nature, Fraser had earned the nickname of The Jolly Octopus. One of the early interests was to form the first firm of stockbrokers in Singapore. In fact it was not until the 1880s, that they identified drinks as being a potentially profitable business, when they founded the Singapore and Straits Aerated Water Company. In 1898, the beverage company changed its name to Fraser & Neave which became publicly listed on the stock exchange.

Fraser retired and died in England in 1907. Neave was born in 1845 in Dundee and he died at Aberfeldy in Scotland in 1910. Neave's estate at Port Dickson in Malaysia was named Drumochter after an area in Scotland close to the Drumochter Pass in the Highlands. Neave lived for a short time at Dunolly near Aberfeldy in Perthshire. Their legacy is a world-wide conglomerate involved in printing, publishing, beverages and property which currently has a market capitalisation of more than 13 billion dollars.

If Scotland is a relatively remote country on the northern fringes of Europe, then the Shetland Isles is its Ultima Thule with its capital Lerwick being over 300 miles north of Edinburgh at latitude 60 degrees North; it is closer to Norway which is just over 200 miles to the east. Sir Walter Scott set his work, *The Pirate*, in the seas around Shetland and travelled there in 1814 to research for the story in the company of Robert Stevenson, an engineer of the Lighthouse Board and father of the writer Robert Louis Stevenson.

In *The Pirate*, Scott describes, 'the deep and dangerous seas of the north, amidst precipices and headlands many hundreds of feet in height – amid perilous straits, and currents, and eddies – long sunken reefs of rock, over which the vivid ocean foams and boils – dark caverns, to whose extremities

neither man nor skiff has ever ventured – lonely, and often uninhabited isles – and occasionally the ruins of ancient northern fastnesses, dimly seen by the feeble light of the Arctic winter.'

During Scott's visit to the islands, he was entertained by the local judge Mr Andrew Duncan where he would almost certainly have met his son, and namesake of the great writer, the young Walter Scott Duncan, then about 13 or 14 years old. Scott does not refer specifically to the youngster in his diary but he does comment on Duncan and gives some vivid descriptions of the islands. Sir Walter Scott's diary entry of 4 August 1814 recorded: 'Mr Duncan, sheriff-substitute, came off to pay his respects to his principal; he is married to a daughter of my early acquaintance, Walter Scott of Scots-hall. We go ashore. Lerwick, a poor-looking place, the streets flagged instead of being causewayed, for there are no wheel carriages. The streets full of drunken riotous sailors, from the whale vessels. It seems these ships take about 1000 sailors from Zetland (Shetland Islands) every year, and return them as they come back from the fishery.' He continued, 'The Zetlanders themselves do not get drunk, but go straight home to their houses, and reserve their hilarity for the winter season, when they spend their wages in dancing and drinking'.

The Singapore River mouth, c 1830. (Courtesy of the National Museum of Singapore, National Heritage Board)

Scott emphasises the poverty of the land and refers to the sheep as 'miserable-looking, hairy legged creatures', and points out that for a Shetland farmer to make ends meet he must turn to the sea. He is complimentary about the people referring to a 'strong, clear-complexioned, handsome race, and the women are very pretty.' He adds that in spite of the poverty of the land, the Shetlanders import significant quantities of 'spirits, tea, coffee, tobacco, snuff and sugar' and comments that the habits of foreign luxuries must have been acquired by seamen in their foreign trips. Tea, he states, 'is used by all'.

In 1823, nine years after his encounter with the great novelist, Walter Scott Duncan left his Shetland homeland for Singapore where he joined the trading company of A L Johnston & Co. Duncan sailed from Lerwick in March and travelled to Singapore via Edinburgh and London which he left on 5 May on the voyage to Batavia which he reached on 4 October and thence to Singapore. We are fortunate to have a diary of Mr Duncan's sojourn in Singapore which gives some insight into the daily life of the traders just a few years after the founding of the East India Company factory in 1819.

Duncan informs us that his wardrobe for the journey and new life cost 56 pounds four shillings and fourpence, an astonishing sum which converted to todays prices would be close to £4,000 or about S$8,000. Of course for a gentleman the correct outfit for every occasion was a must and his journey would no doubt be encumbered with a plethora of cases, trunks and boxes replete with boots, shooting gear, formal dinner outfits and a selection of hats. His passage cost 80 guineas, a significant sum. In spite of being prepared with what must have been a sartorial extravaganza, it was clearly insufficient, as we hear from Walter's diary that within a year he orders from China some replacements consisting of 36 jackcoats, 24 waistcoats, 48 pairs of trousers and one piece of grass cloth for neck cloths. He enterprisingly sends examples of the styles he desires.

Life in the settlement revolved around the arrival of shipping and Duncan gives regular accounts of the vessels arriving and some detail of their cargoes. Much of the diary is also taken with recording the social life, clearly very active. We hear of dinners, breakfasts and drinks in the evening, such as in these entries:

April 14 1824 – on Tuesday last had the pleasure of dining at Major Murray's, Mr and Mrs Read and Miss Fraser. After dinner we drove out in the buggy with Captain Pearl and walked down to the beach in company of Captain Maclean. Invited to breakfast aboard the 'Hastings' next morning.

April 15 – went to 'Hastings' at about half-past-seven, Dr Montgomerie and Mr Bernard also expected. Had to leave the deck because of the heat, invited to dinner by Captain Maclean.

April 16 – Gloomy and threatening day, three unfortunate Malays struck by lightning at Kampung Glam. Exceedingly good dinner, tea on the poop succeeded by a devil*. Landed about nine and then went to Mr Guthrie's and had a brandy and water.

Earlier, he refers to a letter from 'my dear Jessie', unknown but perhaps a girlfriend or close cousin or sister, which has taken a full seven months to arrive from Shetland; letters from home are much sought after by him and his disappointment is expressed when he has not had a letter for some time or indeed when he receives a business letter from home which contains no local news. When he does get news of home he is concerned for the welfare of his fellow islanders, for example, when he hears that the Greenland whaling season has been poor, he records, 'bad news for my native island'. His partner Mr Hay[+], also a Shetlander, who had joined A L Johnston & Co in 1820, reports from a consignment of Scottish newspapers the birth of a son and heir by Mrs F Gifford, of Fairy Bank, Zetland. No clear relationship is established but it shows at least interest continuing in the small island community where most people in business would know each other.

He tells us also of a visit to a junk offshore where they had hoped to be entertained with some bird's nest soup, a speciality which he had never experienced. Sadly, we learn that after being offered some candy and weak tea they discover the bird's nest soup has been consumed but they are regaled with 'cold roast duck, curried fowl, a pudding made with the lights and liver of a pig and a piece of pork swimming in fat covered with dried mushrooms', all of which they ate, albeit hesitantly at first, because of the appearance of the food.

Some days later he writes, 'felt sickish from drinking too much on a stomach at present undergoing a course of medicine,' but in true Shetland fashion he 'danced it away, to the enlivening strains of two fiddlers.'

W S Duncan also comments on cargoes and prices in which opium features quite largely. He expresses concern that certain shipments might have

[+] Highly seasoned or spiced foods or often used simply to refer to supper.

* Andrew Hay was born in Shetland in 1789. His family retained business interests in Lerwick, Shetland, where one of the harbours constructed in 1815 known as Hay's Dock, remained active throughout the 19th and 20th centuries. Hay returned to the UK in 1837 with a significant fortune.

a detrimental effect on the market prices without, of course, expressing any qualms over the effect of its end use. One cargo arriving from Calcutta he commented on, includeed 'Gunahs, Sannahs, Cumas, Gunny bags, Saltpetre, Iron, Household furniture and a considerable quantity of opium.'

In September 1834, Duncan wrote a 'Memorandum of Sundry Goods suitable for the Singapore Market', now housed in the Shetland Islands Archive, which extends to nine pages of closely written copperplate in Duncan's hand. The document was sent back to the Shetland Islands to assist the merchants there who were interested in shipping goods to the East. It is arranged alphabetically and ranges from Anchors, Blocks and Biscuit, through Felt, Guns and Hats, to Tar, Twills, Tinplates and Varnish.

Duncan gave clear instructions on the size, weight and material construction of the anchors and blocks, how to pack the biscuits in airtight casks. Against Beer, he wrote, 'much used, Bass, Hodgsons and Allsops are the best brands', and added that it should be shipped in wood, not bottles. Claret, Brandy and Champagne sells well he continued, but there is no mention of whisky. Guns were also required in the form of fowling pieces and pistols; muskets with bayonets were also of interest. Hams of good quality in quantities of 100 or 200 were thought to sell well and 'They must be packed carefully. Those from Yorkshire are most esteemed'. Duncan's instructions were a complete almanac for the busy trader and outlines the need for almost every sort of commodity in the growing colony.

Glencaird, the residence of John Fraser.

An archipelago of over 100 islands totalling 567 square miles and a population even today at just over 22,000, it is not surprising that the Shetlanders were seafarers and used to travelling the globe but how likely is it that two Shetland men born within a few years of one another, both called Gilbert, would end up making their fortunes in Singapore?

Gilbert Angus, born in 1815 just a few weeks after the decisive British victory over Napoleon Bonaparte at Waterloo, gives his name to Angus Street close to the Singapore River where the infant colony would have been at its most active and vibrant. Angus was in partnership with Hoo Ah Kay, familiarly known as Whampoa from the village near the Pearl River in China where he was born, in a number of ventures including that of an ice house built in 1854 on the bank of the Singapore River at Clark Quay near the junction of River Valley Road and Hill Street. That business turned out to be an unprofitable one and ceased trading.

Angus was clearly a wealthy man and was owner of the White House Park Estate which was a significant 54 acre nutmeg plantation. Houses on this site were built probably by Angus but also by Fraser of Fraser & Neave, including Glencaird where Fraser himself lived, Glencaird being the name of an estate in south-west Scotland. Angus started off life as a lowly bookkeeper but soon progressed into business on his own account as an auctioneer. Gilbert Angus died in Singapore at the age of 71 in March 1887 leaving seven sons and two daughters.

The other Gilbert, Gilbert Bain, a cousin of Angus, also had a brother, Robert Bain who came to Singapore. Both were enterprising businessmen and involved in a range of trading activity. Robert worked at A L Johnston & Co the major Scottish trading merchant. Gilbert and Robert were both members of the Grand Jury and their names appear in various pronouncements of that body.

Bain was one of the founding shareholders of the Singapore Library so the juxtaposition of the National Library headquaters opened in 2005 and Bain Street next to it is particularly fortuitous.

Gilbert Bain was one of a family of 13 from his father's second marriage. Several of his other brothers also ventured abroad: John died in Java in 1842; William was in business in Lerwick, Shetland, but died in Australia; Lawrence also died in Java in 1841, and the tenderly named Philadelphius whose brotherly love did him no service, died in Colombo, Ceylon, in 1852 at the tender age of 22. Another brother George not only joined the renowned P&O Shipping Company in 1844, but married the niece of one of its co-founders, Arthur Anderson, who was also a Shetlander.

Men from small countries like Scotland with few opportunities were always willing to travel to hopefully make a fortune but in the tropics many would not have survived more than a few years. Gilbert Bain was more fortunate than his brothers and many of his countrymen. He lived to a good age and retired with a substantial sum of money. Bain was also an associate of Whampoa, and at one point made arrangements to send Whampoa's son for a holiday to Shetland. What he might have made of the Isles is not recorded but a more different climate and mode of life one can scarcely imagine.

Records in Shetland confirm that he never married and when he died in 1886 at the age of 76 in a substantial house in Mayfield, Edinburgh, he left most of his money to his two sisters who founded, in his name, a hospital in the Shetland Islands capital of Lerwick. The hospital, having moved from its original building in 1961, is still known as the Gilbert Bain Hospital. The hospital carries a plaque in remembrance stating: 'Gilbert Bain Hospital Gifted to Lerwick in memory of Gilbert Bain By his sisters Enga and Isabella 1901.'

The Shetland Times of 28 April 1900 headlined the gift as a 'Handsome Bequest to Lerwick' and describes the gift of £2,000 (more than £100,000 today) to fund the building and a further £1,000 to form the nucleus of a fund for endowing the hospital. The article concludes: 'Such a generous bequest, intended to supply a much felt want, cannot fail to earn the gratitude of the whole community.' In a slightly macabre twist the original building is now used as a funeral parlour.

In records of the time in Singapore there is confusion between Gilbert Angus and Gilbert Bain as the latter referred to himself regularly as Gilbert Angus Bain. Bain's main work seemed to be with Maclaine Fraser in shipping, property and general merchanting. *The Straits Times* carried an advertisment from Maclaine Fraser & Co indicating that from 31 December 1854 Gilbert Angus Bain was no longer involved with that firm.

The newspapers must have been the only reliable place to keep up with who was in business with whom as this no doubt changed frequently as firms formed, disbanded and reformed in different guises. On 3 August 1852, Charles Carnie placed an advertment from Glasgow indicating that he was no longer a partner in any of the branches of Martin Dyce & Co, the Scottish trading company. Carnie's first house in Singapore was called Cairn Hill built in 1840 and surrounded by nutmeg plantations. The Scottish word *cairn*, means a pile of stones, usually marking a significant place or event. They appear on the summits of hills where most walkers will place a stone

Top right: Cairn Hill, the house of Charles Carnie, c 1840s. (National University of Singapore Museum Collection) Bottom right: Nutmeg from the William Farquhar Natural History Drawings. (By courtesy of Mr G K Goh)

thus gradually increasing the size as years progress.

There are few records of any merchants emanating from Glasgow, perhaps its proximity to the west coast of Scotland and its already extensive trade with the West Indies and Americas tended to encourage adventurous traders in those directions. One exception was Walter Buchanan, born in Glasgow in January 1797. His father, Andrew Buchanan, was a merchant trading in the Baltic area of Europe and Walter's first foray into business was to Hamburg, Germany where he took charge of his father's business. Later, he widened his horizon and turned towards the East, going into partnership with James Hamilton and trading in Glasgow under the name of Buchanan Hamilton & Co and in Singapore as Hamilton & Gray. After the East India Company monopoly ended in 1833, the Singapore business started to improve. Walter Buchanan managed the business from Glasgow and became a Member of Parliament. He died in 1883. One of the partners in Hamilton & Gray was George Henderson, so this one trading company alone gives its name to Henderson Road, Gray Lane and Hamilton Road in Singapore.

Singapore is proud of the Gemmill Fountain. Originally gracing Raffles Place and later Empress Place, it now stands in the National Museum of Singapore as a permanent memorial to banker and auctioneer John Gemmill. He donated the marble drinking fountain to the city in 1864. The first public drinking fountain in Singapore, its inscription reads that it is 'for the use of all nations at Singapore'.

Gemmill being a Scottish name, he was mostly likely a Scot. In examining birth records in Scotland from 1750 to 1820 there are just over 20 John Gemmills all hailing from south-west Scotland. The fact that he retired to London is not unusual for many Scots; having some money in their pockets, the distractions of the big city are more likely to lure expatriates than the douce pleasures of rural life in the land of their birth, particularly after experiencing the tropical pleasures of Singapore.

Ann Siang Hill, the small hill in Chinatown which Gemmil owned, used to be known as Gemmill Hill, until it was sold to a Malacca-born landowner after whom the hill is now named. Although the hill no longer bears the name Gemmill, there is still a Gemmill Lane nearby.

There used also to be a Guthrie Lane linking Cecil Street to Telok Ayer recognising James Guthrie of one of the premier trading houses in Singapore. Alexander Guthrie, a Scot, landed in Singapore from South Africa in January 1821 and set up one of the first British trading companies. In 1837, he was joined by his nephew James, aged 15.

The Guthries were from Menmuir parish in Angus. Reportedly born in

1796, there is only one birth record in that year of an Alexander Guthrie, in Menmuir, Angus on 30 December.

Alexander had obtained a licence to trade from Hastings, the Governor-General of India, and with the help of fellow Scots, Alexander Laurie Johnston and William Farquhar, began to sell British goods from a godown at Hill Street. Guthrie, in partnership with various individuals in the early years, quickly became established and both imported goods and traded in local goods acting as a transshipment and storage point. He soon extended his interests to agriculture investing in nutmeg and clove plantations as well as pepper and other spices. On retirement in 1847, he transferred the company to James Guthrie.

Expanding into property and insurance the organisation prospered under James's guidance. Problems of disease in the plantations and estate workers being attacked by tigers were just some of the obstacles which a Scottish education is unlikely to have prepared him for, and would of course be unknown in the famed Angus glens. However, these were overcome one way or another with enterprise and skill as the company continued to grow and expand its interests into Malaya where rubber and later oil palm became important products. In modern times, Guthrie merged with Sime Darby, also set up by Scots, William Middleton Sime and his younger brother John Middleton Sime. This formed the largest landowner in Malaysia and one of the largest companies in Malaysia with extensive oil palm plantations; in 1981 the group came under the ownership of the Malaysian Government thus losing the connection with the land of its founders.

The Simes were born in Fife in the parish of Kilconquhar, one of many strangely pronounced Scottish place names designed to catch out the unwary, in this case pronounced Kinneuchar. William was born on 4 September 1873 and John on 11 August 1878. It is interesting to note that in both cases the Registrar recording the birth was Thomas Sime, perhaps a relation.

There were many Guthries from the Angus glens, the most notable being the Reverend Dr Thomas Guthrie, a noted divinity scholar and philanthropist. He was one of the founders of the Free Church of Scotland and also of the famed 'Ragged Schools' which offered free education for destitute children, both boys and girls. He travelled the world, including a trip to Australia so it is quite possible that he stopped for a brief sojourn in Singapore. He could well have been related to the Guthries of Singapore but it is not established. Guthrie the philanthropist was the great grandfather of Tyrone Guthrie the celebrated theatre director who worked extensively in Ireland, Britain and Canada. Other well known Scots traders involved with the de-

Overleaf: Commercial Square, showing Gemmill's Fountain on the right.

velopment of Guthries include Sir John Anderson, whose family hailed from Rothesay on the River Clyde and Thomas Scott who was heavily involved in the founding of the Tanjong Pagar Dock Company.

Alexander Guthrie, after retirement, lived in London and remained active in support of developments in favour of Singapore by lobbying the East India Company Board and the British Government on matters such as the local currency, maintenance of the free trade ethos and finally the transfer of Singapore from the control of India to the Government in 1867, two years after his death.

A L Johnston & Co was one of the earliest, if not the earliest, trading house in Singapore; it was certainly the first European business. In common with most traders of the time, it covered a vast range of products and interests; if it needed doing then the early traders were up for it particularly if a profit could be turned.

Alexander Laurie Johnston was born in Dumfriesshire into a respectable family. Johnston was a well known family from Annandale as we can detect from an extract from an old Scottish ballad quoted by Sir Walter Scott in his novel *The Fair Maid of Perth*.

Singapore. Johnston's Pier and Collyer Quay.

Picture postcard of Johnston's Pier, c 1880.

Within the bounds of Annandale,
The gentle Johnstones ride;
They have been there a thousand years,
A thousand more they'll bide

Like so many, he left home to seek fame and fortune in the British Empire and first of all travelled to India with the East India Company. When he left the East India Company, he took command of a trading ship and undertook a number of voyages. He started business in Singapore in 1820 representing a wide number of other traders, acting as agents for shipping of both goods and passengers. His reputation was one of good humour, kind, sociable and generous and Raffles became friends with him and appointed him as the first Magistrate in Singapore. Raffles also appointed him as a Trustee of the Raffles Institution and his company as the Honorary Treasurer.

Johnston was highly respected amongst his colleagues in the business world and he was instrumental in establishing the Singapore Chamber of Commerce in 1837 and became its first Chairman. Although he had business associates, notably Christopher Read and his son, William Henry Macleod Read, both Scots, the company name did not continue beyond A L Johnston's involvement and the firm closed when he left Singapore to retire in Scotland in 1841. Read, however, continued trading until the company went out of business in 1892.

The first jetty for landing goods, materials and people, constructed between 1854 and 1856 under the supervision of Captain Ronald MacPherson, was named Johnston's Pier in recognition of his early involvement in the import business and the esteem in which he was held by other settlers. Situated opposite Fullerton Square and close to Battery Road and Collyer Quay, the jetty was demolished in 1933 when it was replaced by Clifford Pier. There was some discontent expressed at the change of name by the business community who felt that Johnston's name should continue to be recognised. The various ethnic communities made presentations to him on his retirement to Scotland. He moved back to the area he and his family were from in Kirkcudbright, south-west Scotland near the Solway shore at Bluehill, Auchencairn.

The trading company Rawson Holdsworth & Co, was founded in 1821. This firm was joined by William Wemyss Ker or Kerr in 1828 and became Kerr Rawson in 1830 when Kerr was admitted as a partner. William Wemyss Kerr was born in Culross, on the north shore of the Forth at that time in the County of Perth, on 2 January 1802. Culross has since been subsumed into the County of Fife. He travelled to Singapore and, in 1830 at the age of 28, joined the firm which imported a wide variety of merchandise and played an important part in the development of the settlement. Kerr was involved in the creation of what became Keppel Harbour and Docks.

In the 1840s, William Ramsay Paterson, born in Perthshire in 1802, joined as a partner. In 1859, Kerr Rawson was dissolved and became Paterson, Simons & Co. Paterson Road is named after Paterson. The business of these groups was similar to the other agencies trading in rubber, cotton, copra and pineapples, amongst other things. The company of W R Paterson was formed in 1842 which then became McEwen & Co in 1849 when Paterson retired. It eventually became the Borneo Company Limited in 1857.

The Borneo Company Limited was established from a number of firms which had Singapore as their eastern base. R and J Henderson & Co of Glasgow and George Henderson of Calcutta joined forces with MacEwen & Co of Glasgow and Singapore to act as agents and traders for James Brooke the 'White Rajah' of Sarawak. Brooke was born in England but his mother was Scottish, being the illegitimate daughter of the Scottish Peer Colonel William Stuart, 9th Lord of Blantyre, and his mistress Harriott Teasdale.

The Borneo Company is an early example of Singapore being used as an import and export trading hub with investors in Scotland and London benefitting from local traders carrying out the actual business.

The Borneo Company also started a motor trading company as well as the Alexandra Brickworks in Singapore. In later years, it was acquired by the Inchcape Group of companies, a major conglomerate which takes its name from the Inchcape Lighthouse some miles off Arbroath on the east coast of Scotland. Inchcape was started in 1847 by two Scots, William Mackinnon and Robert Mackenzie from Campbeltown who met in Calcutta, and formed a trading company of that name. In 1874, they were joined in partnership by James Lyle Mackay, born in Arbroath. Mackay soon became the sole proprietor who, on achieving fame and an Earldom, chose the title Baron Inchcape of Strathnaver, being inspired by the technical feat of the construction of the Inchcape Light. Mackinnon and Mackenzie also founded a shipping business.

In 1867, Samuel Gilfillan established with H W Wood the Singapore-based Gilfillan Wood & Co, later trading as, on adoption of a new partner, William Adamson, Adamson & Gilfillan. One of the partners in this group was the sharply named Scotsman, James Sword, who in 1886, in partnership with German, Herman Muhlinghaus, co-founded The Straits Trading Company to smelt tin. This company exists to this day with extensive trading and property interests. Also in 1886, Archie Charles Harper arrived

Alexander Guthrie and the seal of the Borneo Company.

in Selangor as the first European trader to deal in horse fodder. This company expanded and eventually merged with Adamson & Gilfillan to become the Harper Wira Group which continues to trade with extensive business interests in Malaysia and Brunei.

Charles Spottiswoode, of the trading company and shipping agency Spottiswoode & Connolly, was another Scot who took an active part in developing both the business and social side of the colony. He was a steward at many of the St Andrew's celebrations held annually in Singapore and together with W M Read and William Napier established the first racecourse on the island. Charles was born on 21 December 1812 and, although the genealogy line is unclear, he is probably the 12th child of William Spottiswoode, a corn dealer near Edinburgh. The name Spottiswoode itself comes from Berwickshire in the south of Scotland.

As the early traders were almost exclusively Scots, it is not surprising that for many years they initiated their friends and family into working in the east. Those who ventured to Singapore were known personally, indeed many were family members, to pioneers who had already made the perilous journey and firm steps in establishing businesses.

The Guthrie family, together with the Scotts with whom they inter-married, are a good example of keeping the business in the family as far as possible. In his history of Guthries, *The Traders*, Sjovald Cunnyngham-Brown relates the cautionary tale of a non-family member John James Greenshields who, in spite of being a fellow Scot, a partner by the age of 24, an elder of the Presbyterian Church, the office bearer in the masons who laid the foundation stone of the Horsburgh Light, and generally very active in many aspects of society of the time, was passed over for promotion, went into a sad decline and died in Liverpool at the age of 48.

A picture postcard dated 1909 from an employee of the Borneo Company with its Finlayson Green offices and godowns marked out. (National Archives of Singapore)

Finlayson Green, Singapore

FIVE

The Infrastructure

Trade had to be financed, and the long voyages meant that stocks were tied up for many months in ships' holds and at docksides. During the East India Company's monopoly of trade to and from the East, they were able to generate much of the money themselves but later traders required people to discount Bills of Exchange and provide credit. A number of banks were involved in providing support for the Eastern trade and the founders of many of those were again Scots. Trust is an essential element of borrowing and lending so doing business with people they knew and understood, from places with which they were familiar, would be an undoubted benefit to the early bankers.

Banks
In 1692, John Campbell, born in Lundie, a parish in Angus, just a few miles south-west of Menmuir where the Guthrie family were from, made his way to London and established himself as a goldsmith* and banker in the Strand. He made loans, received deposits and discounted bills as well as operating as a goldsmith. His customers were predominantly Scottish and his clientele included such notables as his clan chief, the Duke of Argyll.

Burgeoning trade with the East would also be financed by the Hong Kong

---

*Goldsmiths acted as one of the forerunners of the banking system in that they were dealing with a valuable material, were trusted and had vaults to store their raw material and products in which others often stored gold and valuables. In 1708, Campbell took into partnership George Middleton, also a Scottish goldsmith. When he died in 1747, the goldsmiths business had declined and the firm became simply a bank. Several years later in 1755, a Scottish banker, James Coutts, was taken into the partnership. James Coutts, in turn, introduced his younger brother Thomas and the banking business, which is known today as Coutts, was established. The banking business flourished in the second half of the 18th century with the opening of trade to India and later the Far East; Coutts Bank continues to this day as a company within the banking group of the Royal Bank of Scotland.

Hongkong & Shanghai Bank on Collyer Quay, 1880s.

and Shanghai Bank, the Standard Bank and the Chartered Bank. All three of which were founded by Scotsmen. The Hong Kong and Shanghai Bank, the initial company of the group now known as HSBC, was founded by Thomas Sutherland who wanted a bank based on 'sound Scottish banking principles'. He was born in Aberdeen in 1834 and educated at Aberdeen University. He worked in a number of businesses and quickly became the Superintendent of the P&O Shipping Line in Hong Kong. He rose to become the Managing Director of P&O at a time of great expansion and directed that company to a pre-eminent position.

Sutherland established his banking business in Hong Kong in 1865. The Singapore branch opened in 1877 in Collyer Quay, a location which it retains to this day. After his return to Scotland, he was elected in 1884 as MP for Greenock, close to Glasgow. He died in 1922.

James Wilson, born in Hawick in the Scottish Borders in 1805, was the son of a textile mill owner whose forebears were sheep farmers in the rural Border country where the clear, soft water and green pastures were ideal for development of the woollen industry. He went south to London and became a successful businessman and was not only the founder of the Standard Bank but also founded the influential weekly newspaper *The Economist* which continues to be published in London to this day. The Chartered Bank was granted a Royal Charter by Queen Victoria in 1853 and was influential in developing British colonial trade, which included the opium trade, in India and the East, developing substantial profit.

Wilson went to India and did not survive the climate and disease; he died in 1860 at the age of 55. The bank he founded continued to flourish, supporting the development of trade to and from India and the East until it merged in 1969 with the Standard Bank to become the Standard Chartered Bank.

The Standard Bank of British South Africa was founded in Port Elizabeth, South Africa, by John Paterson who was its first chairman. Like Thomas Sutherland, Paterson, born in 1822, was a native of Aberdeen. He became a schoolmaster and emigrated to South Africa where he taught and, at the same time, clandestinely founded a newspaper. The newspaper was successful and he later gave up teaching and sold the paper and became a businessman. He never lost his interest in education however, and in later years founded a school for boys which became an elite school in Port Elizabeth.

In 1862, he founded the bank which eventually changed its title to become the Standard Bank and finally, on merger with the Chartered Bank, to become the Standard Chartered Bank which still derives much of its business from the East. Paterson died in 1880 in a dramatic double shipwreck.

On a return journey to South Africa his ship foundered due to a broken propeller shaft and passengers and crew all escaped in lifeboats which became
separated. Paterson's craft was rescued by a ship which later ran aground on
the African shore. In the confusion and attempt to get ashore, Paterson was
killed by a blow from a solid object, possibly the propeller. He was the only
one not to survive the two shipwrecks.

Trade to and from Singapore involving long journeys, uncertain produce, different cultures and a multitude of agencies and intermediaries with
slow communications would not have been possible without the interven-
tion of such banks.

Shipping
The shipping routes to Singapore were made safer by the protection of the
Royal Navy and the provision of charts, lights and other navigational aids
pioneered by the likes of Dalrymple, Ross and Horsburgh. In the days of
sail, the voyages were long and arduous, and the development of fast clippers
taking tea from China to India and on to Britain, to a limited extent, reduced
the reliance on Singapore as a port because the clippers could run the China to India leg non-stop. The development of steam ships however, and the
opening of the Suez Canal in 1869, brought Singapore more firmly back into
the equation as a coaling station.

There were many lines which plied the sea lanes to Singapore from Brit-

Hongkong & Shanghai Bank building, the bank's crest, and Thomas Sutherland.

ain. Two of the major lines were founded by Scots. The Shetland Isles were the home of a number of Singapore traders like Walter Scott Duncan and Gilbert Bain and Gilbert Angus. Some years before they left the Shetlands to find their fortunes in Singapore, one of their fellow islanders, Brodie Mcghie Wilcox left Shetland in 1815 and opened a shipbroking business in London. He took on a fellow Shetlander, Arthur Anderson, as his clerk and by 1822 they had become a partnership trading as Wilcox and Anderson. Their business flourished, amongst other contracts running guns to the Spanish/ Portuguese peninsula under their own flag. In 1836, after taking on some further profitable trading routes they changed the name of their company to the Peninsular Steam Navigation Company. The cessation of the East India Company monopoly opened further possibilities, and routes to the East were quickly added. Thus, in 1840, the word Oriental was added to the company title and routes between Ceylon and Penang, and Singapore to Hong Kong were added in 1844.

The P&O company was no stranger to the shores of Singapore, if for no other reason than George, one of Gilbert Bain's younger brothers, married the niece of Arthur Anderson, the co-founder.

The contracts for mail put the company in an advantageous position with a regular source of income. With journeys from home still taking months, the mail was of vital importance. The settlers themselves, as witnessed by Walter Scott Duncan's diary, would look forward to news from home and the mail ships provided a vital lifeline of communication before cable telegraph systems were available.

In 1847, two other Scots, William Mackinnon, born in 1823 in Campbeltown, Kintyre, and Robert Mackenzie, founded a successful trading company in Calcutta. In 1849, they were joined by two other Scots, Peter Mackinnon and James Hall, and the enlarged business began to charter ships to ply the routes between Glasgow and Liverpool to Calcutta and Calcutta to Australia and China. 1854 saw the tendering of mail contracts by the East India Company and Mackinnon aimed to seize that business. With new ships, he registered the Calcutta and Burmah Steam Navigation Company in Glasgow, a company which became the British India Steam Navigation Company in 1862. New routes continued to be added and in 1862 they were awarded the mail contract from Moulmein to Singapore.

The routes and mail contracts of the P&O Company and BISN Company were complementary and in 1914 the two companies merged and continued business under the P&O name. In 2006, P&O was sold for almost 4 billion pounds sterling to Dubai Ports World.

Background: Map of the region around the Straits of Malacca, 1860.
Top right: P&O wharf, Singapore. Bottom right: P&O postcard.

SIX

Wartime

Of the Scottish regiments the Highlanders are the most renowned, with capacity crowds being attracted each year to Edinburgh's Military Tattoo to witness their rousing display. Few cannot be moved by the sight and sound of soldiers marching through the castle gates under floodlights, heads held high, bayonets fixed, flags and battle honours flying, the swing of the kilt, the skirl of the pipes and beating of the drums stirring emotions by evoking the glorious past of their forebears who distinguished themselves under fire over two centuries in Europe, the Americas and India.

The Scots have a martial culture which emanated, in part, from their belief in a warrior elite and through the intense engagement of the Scottish aristocracy in European wars. T M Devine in *Scotland's Empire 1600-1815* wrote: 'The military architecture confirmed the region's notoriety before 1600 as a centre for murder, cattle thieving, assault and vicious family vendettas which were on a par with the Sicily of the Mafia in the twentieth century. Proficient swordsmen were a common breed in early seventeenth century Scotland. Thus when Europe entered its greatest ever military recruitment boom in the Thirty Years War from 1618, the Scots soldiers were at a premium.' One modern estimate suggests that between 1618 and 1648, over 112,000 men from the British isles were raised for service by different European powers in the mighty conflict between Protestantism and the Catholic Hapsburg empire. Of these, around 60,000 (or 55 percent of the total) may have been Scots. Between 1777 and 1800 alone, the highlands produced no fewer than 20 line regiments for the British army, he noted.

The officer class in particular had been significantly Scottish since long before the political union with England. The British army in North America was only 24 percent English. Over 31 percent were Scots, the rest being mainly Irish and some Americans and others.

Soldiering was a respected option for any young man. The Scots Brigade, formed in 1568 for service in the Netherlands, and the Garde Ecossaise, an

92 Gordon Highlanders, 1846, and the clan Gordon crest badge.

elite military unit founded in 1418 to act as bodyguards to the French Monarchy, were long established units which persisted beyond the union with England. In due course, Scottish regiments were to form the fighting backbone of the British army in fields of battle across the globe. Sir Walter Scott informed us in his Introduction to *A Legend of Montrose*, 1830, that, 'the national disposition to wandering and to adventure, all conduced to lead the Scots abroad into the military service of countries which were at war with each other.' He added: 'They were distinguished on the Continent by their bravery.'

Battle honours gained across the Empire had created a legend of invincibility and 'it was said that the mere appearance of kilted soldiers urged on by the skirl of the pipes struck terror into the enemy'. The martial spirit endured through the First World War whose carnage and catastrophic losses did little to dampen the spirit or the myth of invincibility. According to Devine, 'the Germans feared above all the valour and dash of Scotland's kilted regiments'.

Heroes have no nationality, and if it is chauvinistic to claim a special contribution by the Scots to the development of Singapore, then it is even less acceptable to claim credit for Scotland in that conflict which saw as much bravery and courage in ordinary people as it did in battle hardened troops. But Scottish regiments were represented in the defence and loss of Singapore in 1942, and many soldiers suffered appalling atrocities at the hands of the Japanese during their barbaric rule.

The Gordon Highlanders were raised in February 1794 by the Duke and Duchess of Gordon. Their recruiting grounds were in Badenoch, Strathspey and Lochaber as well as further to the East in Aberdeenshire. The 2nd Gordons were involved in the defence of Singapore, arriving here in 1937 to form part of the garrison.

In the early hours of 8 December 1941, Japanese bombers made their first attack on Singapore. All that month, the Gordons strengthened their defences in the southern parts of Malaya in Johore about 50 miles from the Causeway. More concerted attacks came from the Japanese on 26 January with dive bombs, machine guns and air attacks which left 48 Gordons killed or wounded in the day's action.

In addition to the Gordon Highlanders, the other Highland Regiment which played a role in Singapore was the Argyll and Sutherland Highlanders. Peter Thompson in *The Battle for Singapore*, noted that the Argylls arrived in Singapore in August 1939 with most of the recruits and conscripts from the cities in the west of Scotland in and around Glasgow. Few, if any, would have been familiar with the tropical surroundings in which they found themselves. The driving force of the Argylls, Major Ian Stewart, was their second in command. He started to train his men for the situations they would encounter. He trained them in swamps and jungle country, and created small mobile groups to suit the jungle warfare and tropical terrain they would be fighting in.

Blissfully oblivious to the reality of their situation, the colonials lotus-eating lifestyle was drawing inexorably to a bitter and bloody end. Most officers and senior European officials sipping their gin slings in the officers mess or the Tanglin Club, were unbelievably complacent about what they considered to be the impregnability of 'fortress' Singapore and they dismissed Major Stewart as a 'crank' and his methods as 'barking'.

The British had often promoted a cult of amateurism and held an unhealthy disdain for 'professionals' or indeed anyone who knew what they were doing. The casual deriding of an army officer training his troops how to

Argylle & Sutherland Highlanders crest badge and Second World War recruitment poster.

survive in dangerous and unfamiliar terrain is astonishing and stems from the attitude that the key criteria for advancement are not proven ability but what school you went to and who your friends were. It is analogous, perhaps, to the situation where Stamford Raffles, previously no more than an East India Company clerk, was appointed as Agent to the Governor General of the Malay States and invited to invade Java on the basis of personal recommendation.

Ian MacAllister Stewart was born in India to a Scottish family in October 1895 and was the first officer to land on French soil for the First World War. He was decorated for gallantry for, amongst other feats of heroism, leading a charge of the Argylls from the front wielding a claymore. Stewart argued strongly with the Malaya Command about their tactics which had not progressed or learned from the tragic mistakes of the First World War. The complacency of the high command extended to the civilian colonials of all levels. Lynette Ramsay Silver, in *Heroes of Rimau*, recorded that 'When Major Angus Rose of the Argylls wanted to cut down a row of banana palms to improve his field of fire, he was told that before he could do so he needed written permission from 'the competent authority'. The myth of supremacy was clearly widespread and was only seriously questioned on the loss of the *Repulse* and *Prince of Wales*. These two heavily armed ships, one battleship and one battle cruiser, accompanied by a number of destroyers, headed out of the naval base on 9 December without any air cover. On 10 December, just three days after the devastating Japanese attack on Pearl Harbour, the battle group was spotted by a Japanese reconnaissance flight. Japanese bombers and fighter planes were called in by the spotter and after a one-sided battle, the *Repulse* was sunk at 12.30 and the *Prince of Wales* 50 minutes later with the loss of more than 800 lives. A disaster of major proportion.

On the last day of January 1942, the main forces withdrew from the Malayan mainland, marched through the 2nd Argyll and Sutherland Highlanders positions, and across the Causeway to Singapore. Two Argyll pipers played them across to the regimental marches, 'Blue Bonnets over the Border' and 'The Cock o' the North'. Gilbert pointed out, 'a siege had begun in which superior Japanese numbers and firepower were ill omens'.

While waiting for the others to cross, lying 'on a flat, grassy patch, were the Argylls, all 250 of them, the proud remnants of a whole battallion that had been in action almost continually since the Japanese first invaded Malaya'. Major Stewart said, 'we are going to be the last across'. The Argylls fell in and, led by their two remaining pipers, moved off to the skirl of the pipes playing 'Hielan' Laddie'.

In *The Singapore Story*, Lee Kuan Yew described the moments of disbelief as British forces withdrew from Singapore in 1942, leaving the people in the hands of the Japanese invaders. He remarked specifically on the demeanour of the Highland Regiments. He said: 'Next day, the papers carried photos of the Argyll and Sutherland Highlanders, the last to march across the Causeway, to the sound of 'Highland Laddie' played on the bagpipes, although there were only two pipers remaining. It left with me a life long impression of British coolness in the face of impending defeat'.

On 8 February, the invaders crossed the Johore Straits from Malaya to land on Singapore and, for seven days, the defenders fought against the better armed enemy. The Gordons were defending the north-east of the island when the Japanese landed on the north-west. On 11 February, two days after the Japanese landings, the Gordons were moved to near the Botanic Gardens which was the base of the Argyll's and 12 Indian Infantry Brigade. The Japanese immediately began bombing the base. That night, the Gordons were ordered up into the frontline beside the 22nd Australian Brigade between Racecourse village and the Bukit Timah area. Patrols were sent out and engaged Japanese tanks crossing Dunearn Road. On 13 February, after a short rest, the Gordons returned to the frontline in the Farrar Road and Holland Road area. Air attacks by the Japanese intensified, the much-lauded 15-inch guns were silenced and capitulation came on 15 February. Two days later, the Gordons were marched to Changi POW camp and groups thereafter were taken to Thailand and the infamous Burma railway. By the end of the war in 1945 the survivors were scattered across Southeast Asia and Japan.

In relation to the formal and ignominious surrender to the Japanese, Lee Kuan Yew commented in *The Singapore Story*: 'There were some who won my respect and admiration. Among them were the Highlanders whom I recognised by their Scottish caps. Even in defeat they held themselves erect and marched in time.' Lee also remarked on the spirit and dignity of the Gurkhas who, like the Scots, were renowned for their bravery under fire. Scottish Regiments and the Gurkha Brigades had special ties going back to the Second Afghan War of 1878-1880 when the 72nd Highlanders and the 5th Gurkha Rifles fought alongside each other. It was the influence of Scottish Regiments which led to the introduction of pipe bands to the Gurkhas. The first Gurkha pipe band was formed and trained by the 2nd Battalion The King's Own Scottish Borderers in 1885; all the Gurkha regiments followed suit and formed their own pipe bands, trained by Scottish regiments and led by British officers, many of whom were Scots.

The Argyll and Sutherland Highlanders were created in 1881 when the

91st Argyllshire Regiment and the 93rd Sutherland Highlanders merged. Both regiments already had fiercesome reputations for valour in the face of the enemy. The 93rd was the famous 'thin red line' that faced and broke the cavalry charge of 25,000 Russians at the Battle of Balaclava during the Crimean War of 1853-1854.

As previously noted, the 2nd Battalion of Argylls fought the Japanese on the Malayan mainland and were the last troops to cross the Causeway to Singapore, to ultimate defeat and capture. Of the many who were captured and imprisoned by the Japanese in Singapore – British, Australian and Indian – over half would not survive the brutal treatment, disease, hunger and forced labour meted out by their captors. Military historian Martin Gilbert reminded us that, in contrast, 'German and Italian prisoners-of-war held in Britain, or shipped across the Atlantic to Canada were treated well; none of them died of ill-treatment while in captivity, and none was executed'.

Peter Thompson, in *The Battle for Singapore*, commented that of the British troops, 'the highest losses were suffered by the Argyll and Sutherland Highlanders, who lost 244 men killed and missing presumed dead, and 150 wounded.' The heaviest losses were suffered by the Australians with whom the Scots regiments, in spite of the inevitable rivalry and brawls, always had an affinity.

There are many stories of remarkable survival against all odds whilst in captivity. Eric Lomax, born in Edinburgh in 1919, recounts his personal journey in his memoir, *The Railway Man*, and Alistair Urquhart, also born in 1919, tells his harrowing story in *The Forgotten Highlander*. Lomax eventually comes to terms with his captors and effects a meeting and reconciliation many years after the end of conflict. Urquhart, however, recorded his bitterness at not only the treatment he received from Japanese but the seeming lack of interest by the British authorities of the long-lasting legacy and effect of despicable treatment in captivity. Urquhart refered to the Cold War period when, 'those of us who survived became an embarrassment to the British and American Governments, which turned a blind eye to Japanese war crimes in their desire to forge alliances against China and Russia'. He also recognised and acknowledged that the military prisoners were not the only ones to suffer, adding, 'millions of Asians died at the hands of the Japanese from 1931 to 1945. Like the Allied prisoners, the British, Americans, Australians, Dutch, Canadians, they were starved and beaten, tortured and massacred in the most sadistic fashion'.

When war was declared in 1939, Urquhart was working in the warehouse of a plumbers and electrical merchant in Aberdeen in the north east

Argyll and Sutherland Highlanders training in Malaya, 1941.

of Scotland. His father came from nearby Angus, from which county a number of earlier Scots, such as James Guthrie and James Guthrie Davidson, had travelled to Singapore. Days after his 20th birthday, he received a letter stamped 'On His Majesty's Service' instructing him to report to the Gordon Highlanders barracks in four days. It was the start of an adventure that would turn quickly into a nightmare, but he was conscious of the history of the regiment he had been conscripted into. Urquhart added, 'I would strut around town ramrod-straight and proud to wear the uniform of my local regiment.'

Urquhart, with many of his compatriots in the regiment, was destined for Singapore and more than a hundred years after the first settlers were beguiled by the tropical scents, sounds and sights, Urquhart had his first impressions of the island when he arrived in 1939: 'I caught my first glimpse of Singapore's impressive skyline, like nothing I had ever seen before. Squinting into the scorching Singapore sun, I could see rows of white buildings and dominating them all were the sleek art deco lines of the Cathay Building skyscraper, its spire reaching into the cloudless sky. I could not help thinking of the grey granite of old Aberdeen, wreathed in freezing *haar* (sea mist) that rolled in off the chilly North Sea.'

After arriving at Selarang Barracks of the 2nd Gordons, Urquhart was issued with equipment, including a rifle made in 1907, a pre-First World War relic. His first encounters with local life is interesting – he was fascinated by the colour, smells and food of the East but was shocked and disgusted by the behaviour of his fellow Britons, including Scots, who still made up a considerable proportion of traders and planters, whose arrogant behaviour towards the local people he abhored and vowed not to emulate.

Unsurprisingly, tensions were rife in army life and we are told in particular of rivalry between the Australians and the Argylls which 'regularly spilled over into massive punch-ups and drunken brawls.' But, amidst the build up of troops and the veneer of superiority, even a newly conscripted and inexperienced young soldier commented that despite the importance of Singapore and its strategic value it lacked air power and heavy armour and had a too laid-back approach. Urquhart, in the midst of the attack from the Japanese and shortly after the sinking of the *Prince of Wales* and *Repulse*, was charged with looking after three young Gordon Highlanders who had enlisted as bandsmen; they had been offered a route out with the civilians but as they had joined up as Gordons as they felt it their duty to stay and fight. They were aged 14, 15 and 16 years.

Christmas day in 1941 saw heavy bombing and many casualties amongst the local people and thoughts of the men turned to what things might be like back in snowy Scotland. There would be no celebration in Singapore as the battle raged and discouraging news came of the fall of Hong Kong after a 17-day siege.

Officers and the defence chiefs in London might have held different views but, as always, the men on the ground could read the signs of defeat well before the surrender. Urquhart was brutally honest in his assessment: 'Singapore was lost. But to me it was inevitable that we would fall. All of my previous experiences in Singapore, the arrogance, the frivolity and sheer ineptitude suggested we were no match for anyone, let alone a well organised and determined aggressor'.

Urquhart was taken prisoner and marched with the three boys 18 miles to Changi where his real ordeal began. In October 1942, he was taken by train, with many others, to the Mae Klong river near the Thai and Burma border and, after a 160-mile trek, was forced to work on the infamous Burma railway and bridge over the River Kwai. After harrowing experiences on the railroad, 1943 saw him back in Singapore at a prison camp in River Valley Road where further degradation and brutality awaited. After forced labour in the docks on 4 September in the company of 900 other POW's, Urquhart was put on board ship for Japan. He survived the journey and, on cessation of hostilities, was taken home on an American troopship via the United States, eventually arriving back in Aberdeen on 18 November 1945. He is believed to be still alive today.

Lomax was also born in 1919 in Edinburgh, his mother was from the Shetland Isles whose earlier emigrants to Singapore, such as Gilbert Bain, Gilbert Angus and W S Duncan, we are already familiar with. Lomax would have inherited the resilience of the hardy islanders and their tradition of seafaring, deprivation and tragedy. When he was still a boy, he went to the Shetlands for a months' holiday and, unbeknown to him at that age, possibly played with lads who would be future Gordon Highlanders and his fellow inmates in Changi prison camp and worse.

After education at Edinburgh's Royal High School, he joined the civil service in the postmasters department. With the advent of war in 1939, he was conscripted into the Royal Signals and posted to the military barracks of magnificent Edinburgh Castle. After a short posting to the Orkney Islands, he was billeted in England before heading out to India and, after a two-week journey, disembarked in Bombay from where, after a brief stop in Colombo, he sailed further east to Singapore and thence based in Malaya.

Lomax recounted an officer saying that, whatever happens, the Japanese

would not come through Malaya because it was impassable solid jungle; Lomax commented, once again with the common sense of a young conscripted officer based on simple observation: 'We had seen a lot of Malaya since we disembarked in Singapore, from Ipoh in the west and right across the waist of the country to where we now were, and it was not solid jungle. It was intensely cultivated, rich land, with good and plentiful roads for traders – or for soldiers.' Lomax also refers to the loss of the *Repulse* and *Prince of Wales* as a seminal moment prompting the dawning realisation that defeat was a possibility.

After a retreat through Malaya, Lomax and his unit crossed over to Singapore a week before the Causeway was blown up. He pointed out that the 'streets and roads were full of refugees' who had been forced down by the Japanese advance. 'They lived in tents, under trees, in the fields. No-one knew how many of them there were: someone told me half a million. Soldiers lived in the vehicles they had driven down the peninsula.There was a pervasive smell of decay, ordure, anxiety: the smell of defeat.'

Lomax was working 18-hour days and sleeping on the floor of the command centre in the Battlebox under Fort Canning Hill. Ships were leaving the harbour with civilians, commanders could not give sensible orders because of lack of information on what was happening and on 15 February, staff cars, with Rising Sun flags flying, drove up Fort Canning Hill; Lomax was a prisoner of the Japanese. Like Urquhart, Lomax was forced to walk to Changi where he was imprisoned and, again like Urquhart, his trial was about to begin at Kanchanaburi on the Burma Railway. After experiencing the brutality, back breaking work in harsh conditions and a meagre diet, he succumbed to disease and was lucky to be transported back to Changi camp hospital where he made a reasonable recovery.

After three long years, with news trickling in, the inmates began to hope for an end to their suffering. The fall of Rangoon on 3 May gave them a boost but also gave rise to the fear of reprisals by the defeated Japanese. In mid-August 1945 the Japanese surrender was accepted. On 31 October, Lomax landed at Southampton via India and thence to Edinburgh, his home. Like Urquhart his wounds were not on the outside and would remain with them for the remainder of, in their cases, long lives. Many others from Scotland did not survive.

From the Shetland Isles alone, that lonely outpost in the midst of the northern seas, a number had enlisted in or been conscripted to the Gordon Highlanders:

William Goodlad, Lerwick, Shetland, taken prisoner at Singapore. Died

Facing left: Eric Lomax. Facing right: Alistair Urquhart.

Kami Sonkrai Thailand, August 1943, aged 27 years. Robert Laurence Irvine, Isbister, Shetland, taken prisoner at Singapore. Died of cholera in Thailand August 5th 1943, aged 24 years. Andrew John Jamieson, Peat Haa North Roe. Killed in action Singapore 18 January 1942, aged 27 years. Robert Wiseman, Lerwick, Shetland, taken prisoner Singapore died in West Borneo, 19 June 1944, aged 32 years.

They are just a tiny selection of those Scots who gave their lives in the battle for Singapore. They are all heroes in the fight against barbarity and injustice as are the men who engaged in daring operations Jaywick and Rimau against Japanese shipping in the port of Singapore.

Jaywick was masterminded and led by 28-year-old Captain Ivan Lyon of the Gordon Highlanders in an emulation of the renowned Cockleshell Heroes commando raid on the German occupied port of Bordeaux in France in 1942. Lyon's plan was to cripple Japanese shipping in the port of Singapore and to disrupt supply lines by mounting a special unit called Z Force of Special Operations Australia. According to Lynette Ramsay Silver in *The Heroes of Rimau*, Lyon 'was descended from a long line of distinguished military men whose roots extend back into Scottish history' and whose family shared an ancestor with Elizabeth Bowes-Lyon, the consort of King George VI.

Ivan Lyon was born in 1915 whilst his father was serving in the First World War. After a privileged education, he undertook officer training at the Military College at Sandhurst, thereafter choosing to serve in the Gordon Highlanders. After a stint at Edinburgh's Redford Barracks, he looked for adventure and chose to move to Singapore in 1936/37. Described as having an agile mind, the adventurous and accomplished sailor and sportsman with a wild streak immediately started exploring the region on a yacht.

Whilst in Singapore, he had a magnificent snarling tiger tattooed on his chest, danced the highland fling naked on the immaculate grass lawn of the Air Force Base and, in spite of already having proposed to a girl in Australia, he started to pursue the daughter of the French Governor of Poulo Condore, a small island, used as a prison, to the south of Vietnam. Undaunted by the journey and his questionable navigational skills, he sailed solo and unannounced to the island where his bravado was rewarded by an invitation to dinner by the Governor. His proposal was rejected firstly on the grounds that, 'he drank too much and was far too wild'. However, not a man to accept defeat, he turned on the charm and pursued his suit with some vigour. Success followed and Captain Lyon and Gabrielle Bouvier were married in Saigon on 27 July 1939.

He befriended a fellow Scot, Major H A Campbell nicknamed Jock, a 'bustling bullet-headed Kings Own Scottish Borderer with bright blue eyes and a sandy moustache, who had managed a large rubber estate in Johore before the war.' Campbell enlisted with his old unit and Lyon undertook a number of joint special operations with him. Although Campbell and Lyon were not in Singapore when it fell, Campbell was anxious to hit back at the Japanese and proposed a daring mission which would strike at the heart of their operational base: Operation Jaywick.

On 2 September 1943, the MV *Krait*, named after the deadly snake, slipped out of Exmouth harbour in Western Australia. The 70-foot *Krait*, formerly a Japanese coastal fishing vessel, had been used in the evacuation of civilians from Singapore. It was ordered by Lyon from India where it was berthed. Disguised as a local fishing smack and proceeding with utmost caution to avoid Japanese patrols and taking particular care even in disposing of their garbage, the *Krait* made its way to Singapore, arriving on 24 September.

Of the 14 commandoes on board, six left the vessel on specially designed collapsible canoes and paddled 50 kilometres to Singapore. Just outside the harbour, on a small island, under cover of darkness, they established a base to prepare and launch an attack. On 26 September, they paddled quietly into the harbour and placed mines on the Japanese ships before paddling back to their hiding spot.

Explosions lit up and rent the air and a fearful commotion surrounded the harbour – seven Japanese ships exceeding 39,000 tons had been destroyed. The commandoes waited until the uproar quietened and paddled stealthily back to the rendezvous with the *Krait*. Their deadly job done, they set a course back to Exmouth harbour where they arrived on 19 October after a nerve-wracking close encounter with a Japanese patrol boat. The job had been successful, miraculously with no loss of life unlike the raid in enemy occupied France where only one survived from a group of ten.

The Japanese, believing that a raid from as far as Australia was impossible, and assuming that it was organised in Singapore, took brutal and disproportionate reprisals amongst the local population. The main reprisals took place on 10 October in what became known as the Double Tenth Massacre. The Allies did not publicise the raid in an effort to protect their bases and preserve the possibility of a repeat performance. There was some criticism that no strategic objectives had been achieved but there is no gainsaying the skill and daring of the soldiers led by a Captain of a Scottish Regiment.

Operation Rimau was inspired by the success of the previous raid but, sadly, the outcome was disastrous. Is was also led by Lyon, now Lieutenant Colonel, using similar tactics as with the fishing vessel. However, the opera-

tion was more elaborate and involved the British submarine *Porpoise* taking the men to Maripas in the Rhio archipelago which would be the base for the operation. An Indonesian junk, *Mustika*, was seized and, on 1 October 1944, the junk left the *Porpoise* with an arrangement to rendezvous on or around 8 November. The submarine did not in fact return to the rendezvous point until 21 November when there was no sign of the 23 commandoes who had originally landed.

On 6 October, just before the raid, using top-secret motorised submersibles, was about to take place, the junk was spotted by a Malayan police launch. An exchange of fire, probably in error, set off the alarm, cover was blown and the raid abandoned. Breaking up into groups, the raiders tried to get back to their rendezvous points but Japanese forces and patrols were on the hunt for them. Lyon was killed in an intensive close contact action along with another officer and ten others; after two months on the run 11 men were captured and taken to Singapore where they were imprisoned.

Eric Lomax without knowing any information of the raid, referred, during his second stint in the dreaded Outram Road Prison, to an off-limits area on level one of the prison. He says, 'Somewhere above us, we were convinced, were comrades of ours undergoing a punishment even more extreme than the one that applied to us.' These were undoubtedly the men taken from Operation Rimau.

The only prisoners allowed up onto the floor above were the latrine collectors. Lomax, aware of the 'mysterious and special prisoners up there,' hatched a plot that while he was going up on latrine duty he would accidentally fall down the stairs. This was no altruistic or foolhardy attempt to communicate with or rescue the isolated prisoners, but a brave action to ensure his own survival by getting transferred back to the hospital at Changi. If left for much longer at Outram Road, he knew he would not come out alive: his ruse was successful albeit causing himself serious injury.

Lomax acknowledges the part these men played in his survival. He concluded: 'The silent prisoners on the first floor of Outram Road were men who had attacked ships in Singapore Harbour in September 1943 – just after our arrest – and got clean away, and returned a year later, when they were detected; ten officers and men were captured. They were beheaded on 9th July near Bukit Timah, a bare month before the war ended; they had provided the occasion for my second exit from Outram Road, and I never got the chance to thank them.'

Eric Lomax died in October 2012 at the age of 93.

During the Japanese Occupation, Singapore, like any occupied country,

Top left: Captain Ivan Lyon. Bottom left: The crew onboard the *Krait*.

would be a hotbed of intrigue and discontent; life was harsh for all, not just for the interns at Changi Prison. Chandra Subhas Bose a noted and outspoken politician campaigning for Indian independence, sought to take advantage of the situation and came to Singapore in July 1943. Bose had a Scottish connection in that he had been educated at the Scottish Church College in Calcutta and from there to Cambridge University. The Scottish Church College was a liberal arts and Christian college founded by a Scottish minister and missionary, Alexander Duff, born in Moulin near Pitlochry, Perthshire, in 1806, who arrived in Calcutta in 1830.

Shortly after Bose's arrival in Singapore, he proclaimed the founding of the Provisional Government of Free India, one of whose first acts was to declare war on Britain and the United States of America. With the help of the Japanese invaders, he established the Indian National Army and a number of former British India soldiers, who had effectively been abandoned by the British Army on their surrender of Singapore, were recruited to the cause of Indian independence. The INA failed to make much of an impact on the war and on the Japanese surrender in August 1945, Bose left for Japan. He never arrived; his death in a plane crash in Taipei provoking much controversy and ammunition for conspiracy theorists.

The aftermath of an occupation gives plenty of scope for reprisal, recrimination and accusation of collaboration, and it is not surprising to hear that after the war there was discrimination against Indians who had joined up with the INA. In *An Unexpected Journey, Path to the Presidency*, former President S R Nathan wrote about an experience he had in relation to two Indian senior technical assistants who had been members of the INA. They had been penalised unfairly in a claim for back pay and the resident Commissioner had rejected their claim in no uncertain terms. Nathan, at the time a civil servant in the Public Works Department, referred the issue to an engineer, J R Spence, who asked Nathan to accompany him to the Commissioner's office. Spence remonstrated so forcefully with the Commissioner to the extent that Nathan worried about his insubordination to a superior. Nathan said Spence encouraged him to always 'speak his mind truthfully when something was wrong'.

The case was reviewed and the pay reinstated for the two Indians. Nathan commented, 'This episode taught me to bear in mind that not all colonial officers were unjust and that some would stand up on grounds of principle, if they believed in the cause.' He said of J R Spence: 'I later learnt that he was a Scot and such outspokenness was typical of them, when they saw an injustice'.

A Sleeping Beauty submersible canoe used in Operation Rimau.

AFTER St. ANDREWS NICHT BALL

"GUID NICHT, MON, AND DINNA FORGET ELEVEN O'CLOCK
FOR A JOHN SLING AT GIN LITTLE'S."

SEVEN

Diversions

Wherever Scots go they take with them their culture, interests and celebrations. The merchants, soldiers and administrators who made their way in Singapore in its early days would have brought with them their love of lively music, sentimental song and poignant verse of home to assuage some of the feelings of homesickness to which they would no doubt occasionally succumb.

They would have brought with them their knowledge of clan-based systems and allegiances and common experiences which would draw them together as a regular reinforcement of their nationality. Most of all, they would have enjoyed the sheer fun of a celebration as an escape from the day-to-day routine in a humid climate and still-ever presence of danger far from home.

The principal diversion for expatriates of all nationalities was probably the unending social round of dinners, lunches and suppers. Walter Scott Duncan's diary, albeit covering only a short period of time, illustrates the social whirl of entertaining that assuaged feelings of homesickness and oiled the wheels of commerce. The Resident himself and the captains of the vessels importing and exporting produce were included in the roster of those being 'at home' to visitors for social and festive occasions. Most of them would be living in significant houses with many servants to lighten their burden. The locals, by comparison, would be housed in hovels down by the riverside or in the country, cramped and crowded in unsanitary conditions to which the new residents, including the Scots, would be totally oblivious and uncaring.

St Andrew's Day
The day of Scotland's patron saint, Saint Andrew, is 30 November and although it remains little recognised in Scotland itself, St Andrew's Day is widely celebrated by expatriate Scots with vigour and good humour. Buckley's *Anecdotal History of Singapore* refers to the St Andrew's Day celebration in most years, the first such being recognised in 1835. Buckley said, 'On St

A St Andrew's Ball cartoon from *Straits Produce* magazine, 1926.

Andrew's Day, a large dinner was given by the Scotchmen of Singapore: Dr Montgomerie and Mr William Napier presided'. The venue was the upper room of the Court House. The following evening, a ball was held which went on until daylight the following day. Buckley recorded that the band played appropriate airs for the evening, the ladies wore tartan scarves and the men, inexplicably, wore the 'garb of old Gaul'. This refers to highland dress and is taken from the title of an 18th century patriotic Scots march tune about highlanders in the Seven Years War. The music is composed by General John Reid and is still used today by a number of military units as their regimental march. The words of the first stanza are:

> In the Garb of old Gaul with the fire of old Rome,
> From the heath-covered mountains of Scotia we come;
> When the Romans endeavoured our country to gain,
> Our ancestors fought, and they fought not in vain.

The celebration for 1836 seems to be even more extravagant and ambitious with a public dinner being held and festivities which finally broke up at sunrise after three suppers. Although Buckley does not comment on St Andrew's celebration each year, it seems that a dinner did occur most years. In 1843, the tradition was much alive with a reported 75 attending the dinner offering no less than 14 toasts, including those for the memories of writers and poets Scott and Burns as well as patriots Bruce and Wallace. Also toasted were The Queen, the Governor, President of the United States of America and importantly, the Kirk. In spite of these regular patriotic, and no doubt nostalgic outbursts, a formal St Andrew's Society was not formed until November 1908.

Tradition has it that drink is never too far from a celebration involving Scottish people. Buckley does not refer to this aspect of the celebrations although it is unlikely that Scotch Whisky was absent from such events, nor would the associated inebriation be unusual. Buckley quoted from Gordon Forbes Davidson of Edinburgh who said, 'There seems to be some fatality attaching to clergymen in Singapore, as three following incumbents, all died young and of the same complaint. My own opinion is they were all too strict adherents to teetotalism'.

However, not all were in favour of a good drink to promote health. The Temperance movement in Scotland took root in the 1830s because of concern over public drunkenness and specifically to combat the problem of female mill workers getting drunk and lowering productivity. The zeal

to abjure intoxicating liquor was quickly exported overseas. The Singapore Temperance Society held its first meeting on 26 August 1837. Thankfully, this was not a long-lived organisation. John Gemmill, the one who presented a water drinking fountain, sent out a tongue-in-cheek circular bemoaning the success of the Temperance Society and the consequent loss of trade while, in the same brochure, cheekily advertising his lately imported old Madeira and port.

The St Andrew's Society continues to be an active organisation for Scots in Singapore and anyone interested in Scotland and its celebrations.

A Night at the Theatre

Amateur theatre was another diversion for the traders and merchants of Singapore. Amateur theatre started as early as 1833 and the Scots merchants played their parts in the success and failures of the productions regularly mounted at various makeshift theatres of the day, variously in Cross Street, Ching Long's House in Kampong Glam and in Dutronquoy's Hotel. The names of Napier, Spottiswoode, Read and Dyce appear regularly in the no-

Above: Advertisement for Scotch whisky from *Straits Produce* magazine, 1926. Overleaf: The Esplanade, Singapore, 1842-47, by Charles Dyce. (National University of Singapore Collection)

tices of the plays produced, which include such delightful Victorian long lost melodramas and comedies with titles such as, *The Medley of Lovers, The Haunted House, The Apprentice,* and *The Mock Doctor.*

A Day at the Races

Horseracing was introduced in early days with the first meeting being held on 19 February 1842 near Serangoon Road. Charles Andrew Dyce was the first Secretary of the meet. A race ball was held on 27 February with six of the named eight stewards being Scots merchants and it was a Scot, William Henry Macleod Read, who won the first race, the Singapore Cup, at 11 am taking the prize of $150.

Charles Andrew Dyce, 1816-1853, was born in Aberdeen and was a competent artist producing many watercolours of Singapore, a collection of which is now held by the National University of Singapore. His older brother, William Dyce, was a celebrated artist in Scotland whose best known work of Pegwell Bay, hangs in the Tate Gallery in London; a large collection of his work is held in Aberdeen Art Gallery.

A Round of Golf

One of the first mentions of the game of golf in Scotland is recorded in the Scottish Parliament of 1457, an edict of James II, which bans the game because it was distracting people from the more military sport of archery. The modern game of golf was developed in Scotland although many early versions existed in other countries. In spite of the early start, it was not until the later part of the 19th century that the game began to flourish and grip the popular imagination.

The very early Scots traders did not bring golf to Singapore and it seems that was left to an Englishman John T Goldney. The contribution of Singapore to the development of the game through Dr Montgomerie's discovery of the property of gutta percha and its subsequent use in the manufacture of golf balls is, however, undisputed.

After Mr Goldney's initiative, the Scots got in on the act and one of the early presidents of the Singapore Golf Club was Mr John Middleton Sime whose older brother William was associated with the founding of the rubber, and later oil palm, plantation company, Sime Darby. Fittingly, the road that leads to one of Singapore's premier golf clubs is Sime Road.

The Lodge

The origin of Freemasonry is disputed and lost in myths and legend stretch-

Top right: John Middleton Sime. Bottom right: 14th hole of the Singapore Royal Golf Club, 1929. Inset: A gutta percha golf ball.

ing back to Solomon. However, much of the symbolism, ritual and practice derives from stonemasons of the late 14th century. Scottish Freemasonry, which has its own distinct principles and constitutions, has an ancient history. It is claimed that it was King James VI of Scotland, on his accession to the English throne in 1603, who took Freemasonry south of the border to England.

Many of the merchants and traders venturing to the East would have been familiar with the concept and, perhaps, were even members of lodges before they left Scotland. Robert Burns, the celebrated poet, was initiated as a mason in 1781 and upheld the Masonic ideals of liberty and equality in much of his poetry. His work, 'The Farewell', addressed to the brethren of St James Lodge in Tarbolton, Ayrshire, might have been in the minds of some of the early Scottish masons in Singapore:

> Adieu! A heart-warm, fond adieu; Dear brothers of the mystic tye!
> Ye favoured, ye enlighten'd few, Companions of my social joy;
> Tho' I to foreign lands must hie, Pursuing Fortune's slidd'ry ba';
> With melting heart, and brimful eye, I'll mind you still, tho' far awa'.

The first lodge in Singapore, named Zetland in the East, was founded in February 1845 in Armenian Street, Zetland being another name for Shetland.

The names of the early masters of the lodge include those of the principal Scots settlers such as Read, Dunlop and Napier. No doubt, one of the many diversions enjoyed by the early merchants and professionals would be to engage in the convivial social activities of the lodge, encouraging communication between businesses and strengthening bonds of friendship in a still unfamiliar place.

Singapore's masons were involved in ceremonies of laying the foundation stones of the Horsburgh and Raffles Lighthouses in 1850 and 1854 respectively.

A Stroll in the Park

Strolling in a pleasant shady garden is always a welcome relaxation from the trials and tribulations of the day. Scotland is renowned for its botanical gardens and its history of plant collectors and botanists. The Royal Botanical Gardens of Edinburgh was established in 1670, and the expertise developed in this and other Scottish gardens has been exported to many other countries.

The first botanical gardens in Singapore date back to 1822, just three years after the East India Company made landfall. These first gardens were not designed with leisure in mind. They were a practical approach for testing of crops and how best to tend them. These first gardens with a very business-like purpose were sited close to Fort Canning Hill. It was not until 1859 that grounds were obtained at the current location at Tanglin that the botanical gardens as we would recognise them were established.

In 1860, Laurence Niven, a local nutmeg plantation manager, was employed to develop the site into a garden. Over the next 15 years Niven dedicated himself to this task.

Laurence Niven, also spelt as Lawrence, was born in the parish of Barony on the north side of Glasgow, on 8 January 1826. He was ninth born of 11 children of a family of gardeners. Gardening was obviously in the blood and Laurence worked as an apprentice gardener for the Colquhouns of Luss at their estate on the western shore of Loch Lomond prior to his emigration to Singapore.

His older brother, James Parker Niven, who charted a different path, worked in Singapore for the Scottish trading company, McAllister & Co. It seems likely that he encouraged his younger sibling to move East and join him, and in 1846 Laurence disembarked in Singapore. He worked as manager of the nutmeg estate of C R Prinsep, in the area of the present Prinsep Street.

When he was engaged to take on the challenge of creating the botanical garden, he retained his post at the Prinsep plantation. *The Gardens' Bulletin* of 31 January 1920 comments that Niven, 'was also superintendent of an adjoining nutmeg plantation, so that he could combine the two very well.' He was commended by the gardens committee for 'his taste in laying out the Gardens'.

Niven's original work in designing and establishing the gardens has now been enjoyed by many for over a century and a half, and his classical design laid the foundation for the gardens we know today. The Director of the Singapore Botanic Gardens, Nigel P Taylor states in a 2014 article about Niven, that he, 'was almost certainly responsible for the classic English style landscape design that the Gardens celebrates today.' This design, testimony to Niven's effort, foresight and skill, was one of the principal assets that led to the Singapore Botanic Gardens' inscription as a UNESCO World Heritage Site on 4 July 2015.

The Agri-Horticultural Society continued to be impressed with Niven's work and not only increased his pay but built a villa for him in the grounds,

Botanical Garden, Singapore.

No. 29

now Burkill Hall. Unfortunately, the Society experienced financial difficulties and invited the colonial government to take over the garden. This invitation was accepted but sadly it changed the nature of the gardens to one whose principal purpose was scientific development and evaluation of economic crops; in effect reverting to the original purpose of the 1822 garden which closed in 1829.

This change of emphasis required a trained botanist and, in 1876, before the new director arrived, Niven decided to take home leave. The sea voyage home was long and arduous and Niven was taken ill. Shortly after arriving home, he died on 21 August 1876.

The family were living in Coylton in Ayrshire where there are two monumental inscriptions in remembrance of the Nivens in Coylton Churchyard, the first of which reads: 'James P Niven esquire merchant Singapore in affectionate remembrance of his wife Catherine McLimont Pringle died Singapore 23 March 1867 aged 38; also of his daughters Annie Aitken, died Hillhead, Coylton 19 November 1872 aged 14 years; Jessie Campbell died Singapore 9 January 1874 aged 20 years, the above James Parker Niven died at Hillhead 6 September 1876 aged 56.' The other records, 'In memory of Laurence Niven late of Singapore died Hillhead 21 August 1876 aged 51. Also in memory of his wife Jane Newbold died Singapore 21 January 1906 aged 69 and is interred there.'

Niven's successor, James Murton, took office in 1875 and demitted office in 1880 when another Scot, Nathaniel Cantley, whose parents were from the Islands of Orkney, born in Caithness in the very north coast of Scotland in 1847, took over. Like Murton, Cantley was trained at Kew Gardens in London. Illness in the tropics was a constant companion and Cantley also suffered. Almost immediately on arriving in Singapore he took sick leave. He built on the work of his predecessors but died in 1888 in Tasmania whilst on leave.

At a later date, Murray Ross Henderson, born in Aberdeen in 1899, was a botanist who became curator of the herbarium in 1924. During the Second World War, he escaped to Sumatra and then to Ceylon before finally reaching South Africa. On his return to Singapore after the war, he was appointed Acting Director of the Gardens and became Director in 1949, a position he held until his retirement in 1954.

All gardeners know that their work is never complete and the fruits of their labour will often be seen only by later generations. This is borne out on a grand scale by the beauty of Singapore Botanic Gardens which today are testament to the early work of pioneers such as Laurence Niven. Recognition

Lawrence Niven, Burkill Hall and a picture postcard of the Singapore Botanical Gardens. (By courtesy of Singapore Botanical Gardens)

by UNESCO is a fitting tribute. A further tribute remains in the naming of Niven Road in the vicinity of the plantation where Niven started his career in Singapore.

He died in Ayrshire Scotland the home county of Scotland's national poet, Robert Burns, who penned a brief poem on the 'trysting thorn' in the village of Coylton where Niven now rests. The words could be speaking of the Singapore Gardens which has no doubt been witness to many a tryst.

> At length I reached the bonnie glen
> Where early life I sported;
> I passed the wall, an' trysting thorn,
> Where Nancy aft I courted.

John Thomson, Photographer and Writer

For the grandees of the past, having a portrait painted was one way of impressing the neighbours and creating your own version of immortality. Such paintings were mainly the preserve of wealthy individuals because of the cost of engaging a skilled painter and having the time to sit for the artist. Not so after the development of photography became widespread. After a variety of early techniques involving more science than art came and went, the main thrust of photography took root in the mid-1850s opening the way to any businessman aspiring to leave a legacy of a portrait, carry a memento of family to distant parts or represent scenes of beauty to grace a property. Photographers themselves were interested in this type of work because it paid well and allowed them to get on and do work which interested them personally.

Such an artist photographer was John Thomson, born in Edinburgh in 1837, the son of William Thomson a tobacco spinner. In the early 1850s, he was apprenticed to a maker of optical and scientific instruments and, during this work, he became familiar with the scientific principles of photography. He studied assiduously, winning a prize for English and was elected to the Royal Society for the Arts in 1861, the same year that the Edinburgh Photographic Society was founded of which he would no doubt have been aware.

Edinburgh had a distinguished place in the history of early photography, being the home of David Octavius Hill and Robert Adamson's photographic studio at Rock House, Edinburgh in 1843. Using the calotype process in which they excelled, Hill and Adamson produced a series of portraits of local people and scenes unrivalled in their beauty and execution.

However, Edinburgh held little attraction for the young, adventurous and enterprising Thomson and he decided to join his many compatriots in the East. His older brother William had moved to Singapore some years before and in 1862, John decided to join him. His departure in April of that year started a journey of ten years which took him firstly to Singapore where he set up a studio. His work initially was portraiture of European merchants but his interests took him out of Singapore into the wider areas of the Straits Settlements where he took pictures of local scenes and inhabitants, effectively becoming an early photojournalist recording fascinating and unusual aspects of life.

His travels took him to Siam and Cambodia where he took the first photographs of the impressive monuments at Angkor Wat as well as portraits of the Royal families of Cambodia and Siam including King Mongkut, the king of *The King and I.*

After this first journey, Thomson returned to Britain where he lectured widely and was elected as a Fellow of the Royal Geographical Society. But his wanderlust had not yet been extinguished and he returned to the East. He closed his Singapore studio and moved to Hong Kong from where he spent five years exploring China.

Travelling alone with his dog Spot for company, he courted danger as he sought out parts of China, hitherto not seen by Western eyes, to capture in a series of stunningly beautiful photographs a land, customs, dress and activities which have since been erased by the inexorable march of progress. His photographs are a triumph of skill and expertise and his entire collection from China is outstanding in its scope and beauty. As well as travelling dangerous roads, he had to contend with the technical aspect of photography which involved considerable scientific knowledge. The process he used was based on glass plates and precise chemical formulae to create and develop them. The cameras he used would be bulky and heavy.

In his seminal *Through China with a Camera*, Thomson demonstrated his attainment in personal educational in his use of language, smattering the text with phrases in Latin and French. However much he might try to hide it, and in spite of his gold medal for English, he betrayed his Scots upbringing in using the word *creels* to describe the baskets used by peasants and in the use of the word *cairn* to describe a heap of stones and sod.

He referred little to Scotland, although he did allow himself a little hint of nostalgia in some of his descriptions; he referred to Cheffoo Bay near Shanghai as reminding him of Brodick Bay in Arran on the west coast of Scotland. He referred also in his *Straits of Malacca, Indo China and China*, published 1875, to the local planters getting together in a evening in each

Overleaf: John Thomson and his photograph of Telok Ayer, Singapore.

others houses and on departing to fortify themselves 'and brace the nerves against the attack of a stray rhinoceros, orangutan or tiger,' with a 'dock and dorack* of Scotch whiskey.'

Thomson also describes the scenes in shops and the local traders creating a clear picture with words – albeit without his actual photographs – of life at the time and the position which some local non-Europeans have already achieved and to which others aspire. He describes a large store with the name 'Boon Eng' inscribed on a number of impressive signboards, 'Boon Eng himself accosts you, and invites you to inspect his varied assortment of the choicest European wares. He suggests that you should be good enough to sample his sherry or eau-de-vie (brandy), as they are of number one brands, while his stationery, hosiery and saddlery, are, he assures you, by the best English manufacturers. A fine specimen of the Anglo-Chinese shopkeeper is Boon; tall and portly withal; but while he courts your patronage, you find yourself instinctively turned towards the splendid carriage and pair which has just drawn up at his door; and your surprise is great when Boon Eng himself – for it is just closing time – lights a cigar, steps into the vehicle, and is driven swiftly off by his Malay coachman to some pleasant villa in the country. The coolies by this time are leaving their work, and even among them one sees many who, naked as they are, do not despair one day of wearing a silken jacket and riding in a carriage like Boon.'

Thomson also paints an idyllic picture of the evening perambulations of the well-heeled residents of Singapore: 'The Esplanade runs round a large enclosure of fine green turf – a convenient cricket field and recreation ground – while the road itself forms a fashionable resort where in the cool of the evening, and in a double row of carriages, the wives and families of the residents move continuously in opposite directions for one or two hours at a time. In these daily circumgyrations we not only meet our acquaintances, and exchange nods of recognition, but enjoy the gentle exercise and the fresh sea breeze, which are so essential to good health in the tropics.'

A less idyllic scene, but equally descriptive in Thomson's eloquent prose, are events on the dockside where the 'dark statuesque-looking Kling from the Malabar coast' wait by their gharries or horse-drawn cabs in the hope of a hire. If thwarted in plying for a customer we hear that they, 'seldom if ever resort to blows, but their language leaves nothing for the most vindictive

---

* A poor Anglicisation of the Gaelic, *Deoch an Dorais*, the traditional name given to a drink of whisky on departing a gathering of friends. Literal meaning, drink of the door. Today, Scotch whisky is without an 'e' whereas Irish whiskey has an 'e'.

spirit to desire. Once at the landing-places I observed a British Tar [sailor] come ashore for a holiday. He was forthwith beset by a group of Kling gharry-drivers; and finding that a volley of British oaths was as nothing when pitted against the Kling vocabulary, and that no half dozen of them would stand up like men against his huge iron fists, he seized the nearest man, and hurled him into the sea.'

Thomson also refers to other diversions. 'The Singapore residents have devised many amusements for themselves. They have their clubs, their bowling alleys and fives courts and their racecourse. Picnics are numerous, and the frequent gatherings at private houses are pleasantly diversified by performances at the Theatre, and concerts in the Town Hall'.

Thomson remained in Singapore for a period of about three years during which time he must have made many photographs of locals, the scenes and sights. Sadly, very few of his works from this period have survived. It is quite possible that, on leaving Singapore, his glass plate negatives were sold and subsequently lost or destroyed.

Writing just a year or two before Thomson, the naturalist Alfred Russel Wallace who visited Singapore several times between 1854 and 1862 also refers to the local businessmen in his seminal book, *The Malay Archipelago*: 'The Chinese merchant is generally a fat round-faced man with an important and business-like look. He wears the same style of clothing (loose white smock, and blue or black trousers) as the meanest coolie, but of finer materials, and is always clean and neat; and his long tail tipped with red silk hangs down to his heels. He has a handsome warehouse or shop in town and a good house in the country. He keeps a fine horse and gig, and every evening may be seen taking a drive bareheaded to enjoy the cool breeze. He is rich, he owns several retail shops and trading schooners, he lends money at high interest and on good security, he makes hard bargains and gets fatter and richer every year.' Wallace, who was born in Wales, was of Scottish ancestry, and his father claimed a connection to the famous Scottish patriot William Wallace.

EIGHT

Reflections

Whatever the wrongs are of colonialism, and they are plentiful, there is no denying the spirit of the first generation of men and women who travelled far from home to establish what they regarded as a civilising venture and one which would also make them rich. Not all, of course, became rich and many died of obscure tropical diseases and infections, sometimes on the journey outwards or within weeks of arriving in Singapore.

The pioneers were tough, disciplined, imaginative, self reliant, generous and had a vision of making the world a better place however misguided that might now seem. They created something out of nothing and had to be enterprising and adaptable to circumstances which few of them had ever before experienced. They were, above all, multi-talented. Doctors engaged in business, administrators doubled up as botanists and naturalists, soldiers and engineers were skilled artists and humorous writers and most were linguists with many having an ability to speak not only the principal languages but also many of the dialects of the region.

As well as establishing businesses they built churches, schools and libraries and funded these from their own pockets. They sailed, raced horses, participated in theatrical productions and took dinner and suppers in each others houses in an endless social round. And, no doubt, they complained about the government.

The success of Singapore came quickly partly due to the enterprise of these first colonial settlers, the overwhelming majority of whom were Scots, and largely because of the local people themselves, the influx of traders from surrounding lands and, of course, the well-chosen strategic position of the settlement. The myth of superiority and invincibility which Europeans nurtured was baseless from the start but was only obvious to all from 1942 which signalled the beginning of the end for the colonial adventure.

Andrew Carnegie's adage that because the second generation of business men are never as good as their father's, they should give their money to

The Singapore Girl Pipers march past during Singapore's 1967 National Day Parade.

234 | FROM KILTS TO SARONGS

good causes, can be applied equally to the business of Empire and colonialism. Inevitably, there will be a decline in the principle and ability of later generations but some examples stand out over the past century or so since the representatives of the Honourable East India Company set foot on Singapore in January 1819.

William Farquhar, in spite of the derision from Raffles and his vindictive brother-in-law, did his best to understand the culture by learning the language and dressing like the locals; John Thomson, the photographer and writer, had much of the same attitude some 40 years later when, to succeed in his intrepid explorations in the region, he would demonstrate through his writing and photography an extraordinary empathy with the native people.

Thomson incisively referred to the 'debasing effect on weak natures' of servants meeting every need and he derides his countrymen for using, and often abusing, their domestic staff. Thomson commented on the effect on young people whose, 'tropical education rapidly extends to requiring the most contemptible services from long-suffering domestics. When they have acquired a smattering of the Malay patois, they indulge in vulgar abuse, or assume a tone of injured forbearance; and the keynote of their complaints is Boy! What have I done that you neglect to relieve me of my boots and coat, prepare my bath, or help me to bed, administer a sherry and bitters when I seem languid, or a cocktail (an American drink) at seasons of prostration?'

Over a century after the European founding of the settlement, soldiers like Urquhart and Lomax in the Second World War witnessed the cumulative effect of this easy life on the second and third generations of colonials who did not have the backbone, skill and drive of their forebears. They comment on the arrogant behaviour of their compatriots and their appalling lack of understanding of the situation facing them in 1942.

Like Lomax and Urquhart, Malcolm MacDonald the diplomat and politician, shunned the typical expatriate scene and preferred to mix with local people. Similarly, J R Spence the engineer, impressed former President Nathan with his principled and outspoken stand in relation to two Indian workers. Farquhar, Thomson, Lomax, Urquhart, MacDonald and Spence illustrate across the years that some Scots still held to their history of fairness and belief in 'A man's a man for a' that'.

The Scots have left a significant legacy in place names, monuments, bridges, and ironwork; these are the physical memorials of the Scottish contribution to the 'founding' of Singapore. Through their interest in education, their self-reliant nature, their religious faith, their belief in hard work and industry, they also created a community which would leave an equally positive but less tangible legacy based on their belief in the innate ability of anyone, regardless of their background, to succeed should they have the will.

In Singapore's public memory, the credit for the 'founding' of Singapore remains firmly with Sir Stamford Raffles. His place in history is assured through the creation of a myth and a brand permeated throughout Singapore which is unlikely to be devalued. As Tim Hannigan related in *Raffles and the British invasion of Java*, 'Raffles remains like a rash all over Singapore, his name immortalised in schools, hotels and hospitals.'

In spite of his humble beginnings, Raffles set the guidelines for the development of a new settlement but he was strongly influenced and supported by the ubiquitous Scots. If there was a founding tree which was cut down, it would reveal a St Andrew's Cross at its heart.

Raffles's doctor, Dr Montgomerie, was a Scot. His first two Residents in Singapore, Farquhar and Crawfurd, were Scots. His first patron in the East India Company, Lord Minto, was a Scot. His friend, fellow orientalist and mentor, John Leyden, was a Scot. His ideas on education and the founding of the Raffles Institution were taken from Dr Milne and Dr Morrison, both Scots. His eventual conversion to the benefits of a 'free port' was from Dalrymple, another Scot. And his knowledge of natural history was informed by William Farquhar, whose discoveries he unashamedly took as his own.

The Scots legacy also extends to a number of major business conglomerates whose small beginnings created a foundation for later prosperity which continue to trade principally to this day in the East. Guthrie, one of Singapore's first trading companies, Fraser & Neave whose ownership is now based in Thailand, P & O Shipping in Dubai where the gold is almost as plentiful as the sands, Sime Darby in Malaysia, and the banking empires of Standard Chartered and HSBC which remain in strong positions by sticking to 'sound Scottish banking principles' of which sadly some banks at home have lost sight.

The majority of the Scots described in this volume made their contribution to the development of Singapore when it was an East India Company outpost and then as a British colony. Many of those pioneers laid firm foundations for the early development of the city settlement. One Scot, however, in more recent times helped to pave the way for the transition of Singapore from a colony to its present status as an independent nation.

The transfer to an independent country was fraught with dangers and difficulties. Agitation by political enemies within and outside the new state was compounded by economic problems both domestically and in the region. The new country required robust governance and a major contributor

Overleaf: Road signs bearing the names of Scottish pioneers.

Bain St

MacPherson Rd

P

oldstream Ave

Bowmont

CAIRNHILL

Dunbar Wal

MRT

SCO

Ettrick Terrace

Yarrow Gardens

Minto Rd

Cheviot Hill

Angus St

Yarrow Gardens

Crawford St

Haig Rd

Claymore Hill

Jedburgh Gardens

Crawford St

Cluny Park Rd

Cluny Park

Burnfoot Terrac

Kirk Terrace

rgh Ave

Paterson Rd

ian Terrace

to creating a solid foundation for this would be an effective civil service. A newly invigorated civil service would require a new approach and systematic training. In his memoirs, *The Singapore Story*, Lee Kuan Yew referred to the decision to set up a study centre to teach and develop top-ranking civil servants. He added, 'We chose George Thomson to run the centre. Thomson was in his 40s. He had a good mind, was well read, and was an earnest speaker in his strong Scots accent.'

In 1960, at a time when suspicion of the motives of British officials and civil service must have been high, Thomson was trusted to take on this key role of training senior Singaporean civil servants who would take on the challenges of the newly independent country. The decision was not without controversy. Lee was criticised by the opposition and Thomson took some flak from his former colleagues. However, Thomson's integrity, ability and commitment to Singapore and its success was quickly recognised and, through his endeavours, he made a significant contribution to those who developed the principles and ideas which underpinned the birth of independent Singapore.

Born in 1912 in Scotland, George Gray Thomson OBE, a graduate of Edinburgh and Oxford universities, was a highly respected civil servant who became a Singaporean. He was the Public Relations Officer of Singapore from 1946 to 1954 and held a number of related posts until independence. His role then widened into Director of Training of the Singapore Civil Service and Director of the Singapore Civil Service Political Study Centre from 1960 to 1969, and was Deputy Secretary for Foreign Affairs from 1969 to 1971. He held a number of influential positions until his untimely death in Singapore at the age of 67 in July 1979.

The involvement of a Scot in the transition to independence is a fitting way to conclude this book as Scotland considers its own position in this regard.

Present Day

The independence referendum in Scotland in September 2014 provided what many see as a decisive result of 55 percent in favour of remaining in the United Kingdom. In politics, matters are rarely that simple and the vote has already sparked a further debate on the governance of the UK itself and how greater autonomy can be achieved and managed without losing the strength, history and essence of being a part of the UK. The new Scottish Parliament, established in 1999, currently has powers over a range of domestic issues including health, education, justice, culture and agriculture with authority

Puan Noor Aisha, wife of the Yang di-Pertuan Negara of Singapore, being escorted by G G Thomas at the St Andrew's Ball, 1962.

over foreign policy, defence and fiscal matters being retained by Westminster. It is now inevitable that further powers will be devolved in the wake of the recent referendum and the overwhelming support for the Scottish National Party in the May 2015 General Election.

Based on the evidence of their contribution to the development of the British Empire and the early development of Singapore, it is not in doubt that the Scots are capable of managing their own affairs. However, independence of a small state nowadays is less relevant to many when one considers the need to treat power blocs jostling for economic superiority with some degree of equality in terms of size and economic clout, as well as managing the effects of international terrorism and regional wars which threaten to destabilise the current world order

The forging of the UK in 1707 has been tempered by common experience and history. Fighting alongside one another in creation of empire and two world wars, joint ventures in trade, combined engineering, academic and scientific achievement, amalgamation of corporate networks and the subsequent movement and integration of families and people in a now interconnected world with almost instant communications and transport, has hardened the alloy of union to a degree unimagined in 1707 – a connection which cannot be disentangled without changing the nature and fabric of its constituent parts. There is still a majority in Scotland which is reluctant to abandon this shared history.

However, a shared history and the practicalities of trade and business do not extend to a shared culture or identity. A determined effort was made in the Act of Union to ensure the retention of Scotland's pillars of culture, the law, the church and its distinctive education system.

The extraordinary flourishing of Scottish culture in the 18th century paradoxically, came after the union. The philosophy of David Hume, the geological discoveries of James Hutton, the economics of Adam Smith, the art of Henry Raeburn and the writing of Robert Burns, Walter Scott, and James Hogg, defined and codified not only Scottish culture but influenced and shaped the wider world.

It is this identity and culture which many people now believe is incompatible with remaining in the UK and it is argued that the approaches to dealing with disadvantage, economic growth, inequality, involvement in overseas adventures and engagement with near neighbours in continental Europe are inimical to the Scottish character and philosophy of life.

Comparisons have been made with Singapore which has been held as an exemplar whose successful transition to independence Scotland might emulate. Although the population size is similar, the circumstances could not be more different. Independence was thrust upon Singapore by its ejection from Malaysia and in spite of the lack of material resources, a hostile hinterland and a decayed infrastructure inherited from Britain, it flourished through a combination of inspired leadership and the sheer grit, determination and dedication of its people. Singapore, which celebrates its 50 years of independence in 2015, is an exceptional country.

Scotland has oil reserves, forests, fisheries and significant industries such as whisky, financial services, oil related engineering and tourism as well as a continuing strength in its universities and a growing reputation in renewable energy would give it a strong foundation. Inevitably however, like Singapore, Scotland would experience tough times after a separation and it remains to be seen how it would rise to the occasion.

EPILOGUE

THIS BOOK refers to the building of Singapore in its earliest days following the establishment of a port by the Honourable East India Company in 1819. Scots were disproportionately represented in the ranks of soldiers, administrators, professionals and traders who left an indelible mark on the landscape and institutions of the fledgling colony.

In modern times the credit for constructing a new country must be attributed to the late Mr Lee Kuan Yew and his able partners. On the occasion of his funeral on 29 March 2015, as his cortege left Sri Temasek and paused at the Istana where he had spent so much of his working life, the melancholy strains of 'Auld Lang Syne' played by a lone Gurkha piper standing on top of the Istana tower drifted across the still air.

The poignant and plaintive sounds of the pipes playing a deeply moving tune with universally known, but perhaps little understood lyrics, cut through the air and tugged at our heartstrings.

> Should auld acquaintance be forgot
> And never brought to mind?
> Should auld acquaintance be forgot
> And auld lang syne?
> For auld lang syne my dear,
> For auld lang syne
> We'll tak a cup o' kindness yet
> For auld lang syne.

The sentiment of these words, written by Scotland's national poet Robert Burns, evoking nostalgic remembrance of past events and friends, together with the Scottish antecedents of the bagpipes and the role of Scottish regiments in making them part of the tradition of the Gurkhas, perhaps closes the circle on Scotland's influence on Singapore.

A piper at the St Andrew's Ball, 1962. (National Archives of Singapore)

ACKNOWLEDGEMENTS AND THANKS

Warm thanks to Prof Tommy Koh who gave me the initial impetus and idea and a lot of encouragement as well as a fine Foreword for the book. I am also grateful to Michael Russell, Member of the Scottish Parliament, a good friend and former colleague, for providing a Foreword from the Scottish perspective.

Others who provided invaluable help include my good friends David Bonnar of Perth who provided photographs of Farquhar's tomb, and Ed Stokes of Hong Kong who read an early draft and gave useful inputs.

I am grateful to Charles Morrison of the East-West Center in Hawai'i for offering me a visiting fellowship in 2012 to research and write this book. Hawaii is a special place of inspiration, not least because some 122 years ago, Robert Louis Stevenson, one of the finest writers Scotland ever produced, wrote some of his best books there, including *The Master of Ballantrae*.

Thanks are also due to the Scottish Records Office for permission to quote from William Farquhar's Will, the Shetland Museum and Archives for providing details of the several Shetlanders who came to Singapore, to *The Shetland Times* for article references, and to Miss Anna Loake, who owns the copyright of the images of Farquhar and his wife Margaret Lobban, for permission to reproduce them. To the list must be added the Perth Library for information relating to the life and death of Farquhar during his retired life in Perth, and to the National Archives of Singapore and the National Library of Singapore for their advice and assistance.

Special thanks to my long-suffering wife Irene who has had to put up with an endless barrage of comments about the Scots in Singapore and how they invented almost everything! She helped to proofread my drafts and made helpful suggestions. Her dedication to her own work is an inspiration and spurred me on when I was flagging.

Finally I would like to express my gratitude to Goh Eck Kheng and Leslie Lim, without whom this book would not have been published.

To all of the above I owe grateful thanks. To none however should be ascribed any faults in these pages; any that remain are mine alone.

TWO CAPTAINS OF THE PRESS GANG WALK THE PLANK TOGETHER.

(Messrs. A. W. Still and W. Makepeace have retired.)

BIBLIOGRAPHY

'Memorandum of Sundry Goods suitable for the Singapore Market',
  Shetland Islands Archive.

A Singapore Zetlander. A letter, *Shetland Times*, 1850.

Abdullah bin Abdul Kabir. *Hakayat Abdullah*, 1849, translated by A H Hill,
  Journal of the Malayan Branch Royal Asiatic Society (Volume XXVIII
  Part 3), June 1955

Barrie, J M. 'What every Woman Knows', 1908.

Beamish, Jane and Ferguson, Jane. *History of Singapore Architecture, The
  Making of a City*, Graham Brash, Singapore, 1985.

Begbie, Peter James. *The Malay Peninsula*, Vepery Mission Press, Madras,
  1888.

Bremner, David. *The industries of Scotland*, Adam and Charles Black,
  Edinburgh, 1869.

Buckley, Charles Burton. *Anecdotal History of Old Times in Singapore,
  1819-1867*, Fraser & Neave, Singapore, 1902 and reproduced by
  University of Malaya Press in 1965

Burns, Robert. 'Sic a Parcel o' Rogues in a Nation', 1791

Calder, Jenni. *Frontier Scots – The Scots who won the West*, Luath Press,
  Edinburgh, 2010.

Ch'en, Jerome and Tarling, Nicholas (editors). 'Sino-British Mercantile
  Relations in Singapore's Entrepôt Trade' in *Studies in the Social History
  of China and South East Asia: Essays in Memory of Victor Purcell*,
  Cambridge University Press, Cambridge, 2010.

Cheong Suk-Wai. *Rodyk - 150 Years*, Straits Times Press, 2011.

Chew, Ernest C T. 'The Foundation of a British Settlement' in *A History
  of Singapore*, editors, Ernest C T Chew and Edwin Lee, Oxford
  University Press, Singapore, 1991.

Cunnyngham-Brown, Sjovald. *The Traders, A story of Britain's South-east
  Asian commercial adventure*, Newman Neame, London, 1971.

Cartoon from *Straits Produce*, **1925. (Private Collection)**

Davis, Wade. *Into the Silence*, The Bodley Head, London, 2011.

Devine, TM. *To the Ends of the Earth, Scotland's Global Diaspora 1750-2010*, Allen Lane, London, 2011; *Scotland's Empire 1600-1815*, Allen Lane, London, 2003; *The Scottish Nation 1700- 2007*, Penguin Books, London, 2006.

Dorward, David. *Scotland's Place-names*, The Mercat Press, Edinburgh, 1995.

Fergusson, Robert. 'The King's Birthday in Edinburgh', 1772.

Gibson-Hill, Carl A. 'Memoir of the Raffles Museum No. 3', Singapore, December 1956.

Gibson, Rob. *Highland Cowboys – From the Hills of Scotland to the American Wild West*, Luath Press, Edinburgh, 2003.

Gilbert, Martin. *Second World War*, Weidenfeld and Nicholson, London, 1989.

Hannigan, Tim. *Raffles and the British invasion of Java,* Monsoon Books, Singapore, 2012.

Herman, Arthur. *The Scottish Enlightenment – The Scots Invention of the Modern World*, Fourth Estate, London, 2001.

Keay, John. *The Honourable Company, a History of the East India Company*, J S Furnivall, Netherlands East Indies, 1933

Lee Kuan Yew. *The Singapore Story*, Times Editions, Singapore, 1998.

Lim, Edmund W K and Kho Ee Mo. *The Chesed-El Synagogue: Its History and People*, Trustees of the Synagogue, Singapore, 2005.

Lomax, Eric. *The Railway Man*, Vintage, London, 1996.

Makepeace, Walter, Brooke, Gilbert E and St J Braddell, Roland. *100 Years of Singapore*, John Murray, London, 1921.

Morrison, Eliza A. *Memoirs of the Life and Labours of Robert Morrison*, Longman, Orme, Brown, and Longmans, London, 1889.

Nathan, S R. *An Unexpected Journey, Path to the Presidency*, Editions Didier Millet, Singapore, 2011.

Noltie, HJ. *Raffles Ark Redrawn*, The British Library and the Royal Botanic Garden of Edinburgh in association with Bernard Quaritch Ltd, 2009.

Ramsay Silver, Lynette. *The Heroes of Rimau*, Cultured Lotus, Singapore, 2001.

Reid, Harry. *Reformation, The Dangerous Birth of the Modern World*, Saint Andrew Press, Edinburgh, 2009.

Reith, GM. *Handbook to Singapore 1892*, Oxford University Press, Singapore, 1985.

Sangster, David. *Women of Moray,* Luath Press, Edinburgh, 2012.

Schelander, Bjorn. *Singapore A History of the Lion City*, Centre for Southeast Asian Studies, University of Hawai'i, 1998.

Scott, Walter. *Diaries, Rob Roy, Fair Maid of Perth, The Two Drovers, The Pirate, Heart of Midlothian.*

Southey, Robert. *Journal of a Tour of Scotland 1819*, unpublished manuscript, Institution of Civil Engineers.

Stevenson, Robert Louis. *The Beach at Falesa. Diaries and Letters.*

Tan, Kevin (editor). *Spaces of the Dead*, Ethos Books for Singapore Heritage Society, Singapore, 2011.

Thompson, Peter. *The Battle for Singapore*, Piatkus Books, London, 2005.

Thomson, John. *The Strait of Malacca, Indo-China and China: Or, Ten Years' Travels, Adventures, and Residence Abroad*, S. Low, Marston, Low, and Searle, London, 1875; *Through China with a Camera*, Constable, London, 1898.

Turnbull, C M. *Dateline Singapore, 150 Years of The Straits Times*, Times Editions, 1995, Singapore.

Underneath the Banner – The History of the Boys' Brigade in Singapore, Marshall Cavendish International (Asia), Singapore, 2013.

Urquhart, Alistair. *The Forgotten Highlander*, Little, Brown, London, 2010.

Vibart, H M. *Military History of the Madras Engineers and Pioneers from June 1743 to the present*, WH Allen and Co, London, 1891.

Wallace, Alfred Russel. *The Malay Archipelago*, Macmillian, London, 1869.

INDEX

Drinking fountain in Raffles Hotel, formerly in front of Orchard Road Market. (Photo: Graham Berry)

ABOUT THE AUTHOR
Born in Edinburgh, Graham Berry was the chief executive officer of the Scottish Arts Council until 2007 when he moved to Singapore. In Singapore, he serves on several not-for-profit boards including the Substation and Glasgow School of Arts (Singapore).
He is the author of *Care, Diligence and Skill*, a handbook on governance of arts organisations. A member of the Institute of Chartered Accountants of Scotland, he has worked in financial services in the City of London prior to his senior roles in arts management.

Above: Cartoon from *Straits Produce*, Vol. VI. (Private Collection)

Published by
Landmark Books Pte Ltd
5001 Beach Road, 02-73/74
Singapore 199588

ISBN 978-981-4189-65-1

Printed in Singapore